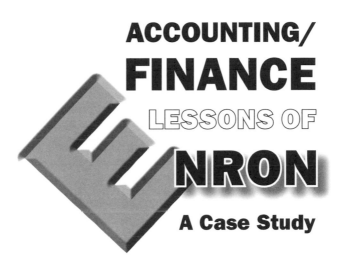

ACCOUNTING/
FINANCE
LESSONS OF
NRON

A Case Study

ACCOUNTING/
FINANCE
LESSONS OF
NRON
A Case Study

Harold Bierman, Jr.

Cornell University, USA

NEW JERSEY · LONDON · SINGAPORE · BEIJING · SHANGHAI · HONG KONG · TAIPEI · CHENNAI

Published by

World Scientific Publishing Co. Pte. Ltd.

5 Toh Tuck Link, Singapore 596224

USA office: 27 Warren Street, Suite 401-402, Hackensack, NJ 07601

UK office: 57 Shelton Street, Covent Garden, London WC2H 9HE

British Library Cataloguing-in-Publication Data
A catalogue record for this book is available from the British Library.

ACCOUNTING/FINANCE LESSONS OF ENRON
A Case Study

ISBN-13 978-981-279-030-9
ISBN-10 981-279-030-6

Typeset by Stallion Press
Email: enquiries@stallionpress.com

Printed in Singapore by World Scientific Printers

Contents

Introduction

There is a major problem in writing this book. To tell the story fairly, a very large number of complexities must be explained. For example, Chapter 2 discusses Enron's Year 2000 Annual Report. It is difficult to study that report and conclude that the firm is heading toward collapse. On the other hand, it is not difficult to identify footnotes that are vague and incomplete (of course, the author also has the benefit of hindsight).

Why write a casebook describing and evaluating events about which there have been criminal trials and extensive hearings?

First, we should review what a manager or financial analyst should have known about Enron based on publicly available accounting information. Second, the Powers Report (William Powers was the Chairman of the Special Investigation Committee of the Enron Board of Directors) provides us with a good foundation for understanding the accounting and financial decisions that contributed to Enron's collapse. Third, the Skilling–Lay Trial enables us to determine the worst aspects of Enron's actions, and gives us a chance to evaluate the Government's conduct of that trial.

To determine whether or not the Skilling–Lay trial was fair, it is important that we understand why the seventh largest US Corporation collapsed in 2001. Why did a profitable corporation with an apparently strong balance sheet go from a firm with profitable growth prospects to a bankrupt shell in a matter of less than 8 weeks (from mid-October to mid-December 2001)?

Even after restarting the accounting incomes of 1997–2001 in October 2001, Enron made over $2 billion of net income over that four-year period. The accounting results of operations do not, by themselves, lead to a forecast of financial insolvency.

I have tried to explain the accounting and financial complexities of Enron and the Skilling–Lay trial as clearly as I could. But unfortunately, considerable complexity and confusion still remain. You should ask yourself — to what extent the accounting and financial complexities were likely to have been understood by Enron's senior management, by financial analysts, and by the Skilling–Lay jury? Also, were Skilling and Lay given a fair trial? Should the objective of the US Attorneys be to gain convictions or to seek justice? Does it matter to the society how a conviction is obtained?

One obvious conclusion to most readers would be that there should have been more effective limits placed on the complexity and opaqueness of the financial transactions and the accounting reports by Enron's top management. It would seem that by 1997, few if any managers or members of the Board of Directors at Enron truly and fully understood the financial transactions and the accounting implications as well as the legal aspects of those transactions. There should have been better accounting disclosures, but equally important Enron management should have made better financial decisions.

I hope this book will enlighten a wide range of readers including those who are not accounting–finance experts. It is also designed to be used in either an advanced accounting or finance college course as a supplement or the core component of a course. Enron supplies many useful lessons. The collapse need not have happened.

Harold Bierman, Jr.
Cornell University
Ithaca, New York

Acknowledgments

My friends and colleagues, Ed. Altman, Dick Conway, Bob Frank, Jerry Hass, and Sy Smidt read early drafts and parts of this manuscript and rectified many errors.

Don Schnedeker, head librarian of the Johnson School supplied ready and cheerful assistance.

Barb Drake cheerfully typed many drafts.

Thanks to all of them mentioned above and many others.

Chapter 1

The Enron Success and Failure

In 1984, Kenneth L. Lay became the Chief Executive Officer of Houston Natural Gas Corporation, a pipeline operator. Soon after he took position, his firm merged with Internorth, another pipeline company. Lay became the CEO of the merged firm, and the name of the firm was changed to Enron. As deregulation of energy became more widespread (Lay influenced the rate of change) the mission of Enron widened to include the trading of energy contracts.

Shortly after the merger with Internorth, Lay hired the consulting firm, McKinsey & Co., to help develop a business strategy for Enron. One of the consultants assigned to the Enron study was Jeffrey Skilling. Lay subsequently hired Skilling to develop new business activities for Enron. Skilling successfully launched Enron's highly profitable business of trading energy derivatives.

Andrew Fastow was hired by Enron in 1990 from Continental Illinois Bank in Chicago and was appointed Chief Financial Officer (CFO) of Enron in 1998. Fastow was thought to complement Skilling's interests and abilities. Appointing Fastow as CFO was Enron's second biggest mistake (it probably would not have been made if the first mistake of allowing the departure of Rich Kinder had not been made).

1

Rich Kinder

In November 1996, Enron announced that Rich Kinder was leaving Enron. Shortly before that announcement the Enron Board of Directors (and Ken Lay) had failed to appoint Kinder as the CEO. The decision not to appoint Kinder as the President of Enron had very little to do with Kinder's acknowledged managerial abilities.

Kinder was (and is) a world-class manager, one of the few effective hands-on managers at Enron. The departure of Kinder was the most significant negative event for Enron during the 1990s. It would likely have been a different firm in 2001 if he had stayed.

When he left, Kinder bought from Enron the Liquids Pipeline Division for $40 million. With Bill Morgan and the $40 million pipeline he formed Kinder Morgan Corporation.

Kinder Morgan went public, but in 2006 Kinder and Morgan took the firm private (the corporation had a market cap of $14 billion).

In 2006, Rich Kinder was one of the world's richest persons and will be even richer when Kinder Morgan goes public again.

The $14 billion of Kinder Morgan value could possibly have been value-added to Enron if Kinder had not been rejected as CEO. Enron needed effective managers of real assets, and Kinder was among the best.

John Wing

John Wing was another great manager (of power plants) who was shown the door by Enron in July 1991. He helped execute the original deal that created Enron and was in and out of Enron from the early-1980s to 1991. He made money for Enron with hard assets.

His biggest moneymaker for Enron was a power plant in England called Teesside. He also did many other profitable deals for Enron.

John Wing did not fit easily into the Enron management structure. He was not the type of person with whom Ken Lay felt comfortable. When Wing wanted to separate his power group from Enron and form a separate publicly owned corporation, Lay facilitated his departure from Enron.

It is interesting to conject what would have happened if Enron had financed Rich Kinder's gas pipeline company and John Wing's power company. These two entities certainly would have developed into two very interesting merchant assets.

The Year 2001

In the year 2001, Enron was the seventh largest US Corporation (based on revenues) and possibly would have been ranked larger if the revenues of all the subsidiaries and special-purpose entities (SPEs) were factored into the calculation. It would have been ranked much lower if trading transactions were not treated as revenue. Interestingly, Enron was ranked number five in the Fortune 500 listing for 2001, published in March 2002. But no matter where we exactly rank it, Enron was a large profitable corporation before October 2001. If we consider only the available public information as of August 2001, it was a very profitable corporation.

On 17 December 2001, the Enron Corporation filed an 8-K report with the Securities and Exchange Commission (SEC). It stated that on *"December 2, 2001, Enron Corp. (the "Company") and certain other subsidiaries of the Company (collectively, the "Debtors") each filed voluntary petitions for relief under chapter 11 of title 11 of the United States Code (the "Bankruptcy Code") in the United States Bankruptcy Court for the Southern District of New York..."*

Thus, in December 2001, Enron filed for bankruptcy. How did a seemingly healthy, profitable corporation transform itself into the biggest corporate scandal of the new millennium?

The newspapers have reported extensively on the clienteles that have been harmed by the Enron collapse. These include:

Employees with 401-K plans heavily (or exclusively) invested in Enron stock;

Employees who have lost their jobs at Enron;

Employees and investors who held worthless Enron stock;

Debtholders who owned debt that had lost most of its value (including bank debt).

But, the list of those affected greatly is much longer, including:

Top management with reputations in shatters and significant reductions in wealth.

Arthur Anderson — A once highly respected public accounting firm was struggling to stay afloat and subsequently was forced to shut down operations.

Security analysts who recommended Enron stock.

Bond rating agencies who had imperfect crystal balls.

Politicians who accepted donations from Enron.

At the beginning of 2001, Enron's common stock was high compared to its earnings. How does a CEO manage a company whose stock is overvalued? Enron management chose to take actions that presented a sunny smile to the public while painful events occurred. There were some executives who, fooled by the firm's own accounting and financial tricks, actually thought things were bright.

Five Business Segments

Enron was divided into five different specific business segments and a sixth general unit (catch-all).

1. *Transportation and Distribution.* This segment included regulated industries (e.g., electric utility operations), interstate transmission of natural gas, and the management and operation of pipelines.
2. *Wholesale Services.* This included a large portion of Enron's trading operations, energy commodity sales and services, and financial services of wholesale customers, and the development and operation of energy-related assets (such as power plants and natural gas pipelines).
3. *Retail Energy Services (Enron Energy Services or EES).* Sales of energy-related products (including expertise) to end-use customers (including commercial and industrial firms). On 30 June 2001, Enron had 730,000 retail customers.

4. *Broadband Services.* Construction and management of fiber-optic networks; the marketing and management of bandwidth; trading bandwith.
5. *Exploration and Production.* Exploration and production of natural gas and crude oil.
6. *The catch-all segment.* This included water and renewable energy; the supply of water and energy to end-use customers, the provision of wastewater services; construction and operation of wind-generated power projects.

The Retail Energy Services and Broadband Services were the two primary problem areas identified by the US Attorneys prosecuting Skilling and Lay.

The Three Components

While Enron was organized into five business segments and a sixth catch-all segment, it is useful in analyzing its collapse to describe Enron as consisting of three basic components:

1. A trading unit;
2. Real assets (generating and transportation);
3. Merchant assets (ownership interests in other firms).

While the initial investment in the merchant assets was less than that in the other two components, it was transactions related to the merchant assets that contributed most significantly to Enron's collapse and to Arthur Andersen's audit difficulties.

Interestingly, the problems associated with merchant assets were created not by Enron making bad merchant asset investments, but rather by the too-clever and too-imperfect efforts to insure that gains in the value of merchant assets that had been achieved were then not lost by value decreases. The objective of hedging the gains was reasonable. The means chosen to achieve the objective by the CFO Andrew Fastow were far from reasonable.

The Enron Hedge Fund

There was a hedge fund (ECT Investments) within Enron that invested in energy stocks. Investments were not limited to energy stocks, but the large gains were made on energy and technology stocks. The operation started small but grew to $150 million of Enron equity, and there were about $3 of debt for each dollar of equity. The fund earned annual returns of more than 20% (*Wall Street Journal*, 11 April 2002). We do not know if the profits continued after the stock market retreated in 2001.

The investing community was not at all aware of the hedge fund operations. Given the large amount of debt frequently used by hedge funds, knowledge of the existence of the fund could upset the conservative common stock investors. On the other hand, the fund offered an investment opportunity (a hedge fund) that was not normally available to investors with small amounts of capital. The hedge fund's income amounted to as much as 10% of Enron's earnings in some years.

There is no reason to conclude that the Enron hedge fund was a material contributing factor to the collapse if this fund is separate from the merchant assets that were reported.

A Distraction

The 11 March 2002 issue of *Newsweek* contains an article titled "Enron's Dirty Laundry" in which it described "sex-drenched out-of-control corporate culture that ultimately wrecked the company". Enron's managerial culture likely contributed to the firm's collapse but in this book let us leave the subject of sex and other cultural considerations with that conclusion. For more details, *The Smartest Guys in the Room: The Amazing Rise and Scandalous Fall of Enron*, can be referred to. This is an excellent comprehensive investigation into the events leading to Enron's collapse. In the current book, we will focus on the accounting and finance issues that resulted in Enron's collapse.

Among the titles considered for this book was *"Enron: The Dumbest Guys in the Room"*, but to be fair, the participants were not dumb.

However, they were not the smartest, and sometimes they were too smart.

Rush to Judgment

In the fall of 2001 and in the winter of 2002, newspapers quickly identified the fact that Enron and the system that Enron operated in were corrupt. Paul Krugman had no problem identifying Enron's corruption (*The New York Times*, 18 January 2002, p. A23).

> The Enron debacle is not just the story of a company that failed; it is the story of a system that failed. And the system didn't fail through carelessness or laziness; it was corrupted...
>
> So capitalism as we know it depends on a set of institutions — many of them provided by the government — that limit the potential for insider abuse. These institutions include modern accounting rules, independent auditors, securities and financial market regulation, and prohibitions against insider trading.
>
> The Enron affair shows that these institutions have been corrupted. None of the checks and balances that were supposed to prevent insider abuses worked; the supposedly independent players were compromised.
>
> The truth is that key institutions that underpin our economic system have been corrupted. The only question that remains is how far and how high the corruption extends.

Is "corruption" an accurate and fair description of Enron's activities?

Bob Herbert (*The New York Times*, 17 January 2002, p. A29) saw the Enron debacle as an opportunity to attack deregulation:

> The kind of madness that went on at Enron could only have flourished in the dark. Arthur Andersen was supposed to have been looking at the books, but the vast shadows cast by the ideology of deregulation allowed that

company to escape effective scrutiny as well. So you have revolving-door abuses and pernicious financial arrangements between companies like Enron and auditors like Andersen that are similar to those between private companies.

There is also the observation of Senator Peter G. Fitzgerald of Illinois:

> Mr. Lay is perhaps the most accomplished confident man since Charles Ponzi.
>
> (*The New York Times*, 17 February 2002, p. 52)

Are the observers fair in reaching the above conclusions? Was Lay a confident man when compared to Charles Ponzi? Could Lay receive a fair trial given the press coverage?

The Activities of Kenneth L. Lay

The 4 February 2002 issue of *Newsweek* had an article on Lay. For the purposes of this book, the pictures accompanying the text are most significant since they give us some insight how he spent his time as the top manager of Enron.

a. Lay with George and Barbara Bush at an economic summit.
b. Lay with Phil and Wendy Gramm (at the 1992 Republican Convention). Phil was a US Senator.
c. Lay golfing with Bill Clinton, Gerald Ford, and Jack Nicholas.
d. Lay with George W. Bush.
e. Lay with Clyde Drexler and Rudy Tomjanovich (one-time basketball luminaries).
f. Lay receiving an award from the Wildlife Conservation Society.
g. Lay with Mikhail Gorbachev.
h. Lay on vacation.

While these pictures prove little, they do indicate that Lay took his public relations responsibilities seriously. There is little evidence to date (including the 2006 trial) that he was a "confident man" when compared to Charles Ponzi. There is some evidence to show that he did not pay attention to the details of the management, because of which he failed to perform properly as CEO. This is particularly valid since the "details" of Enron were material and affected its very existence.

The Path of the Enron Stock Price

In August 2000, the Enron common stock sold in excess of $90 per share. In January and February 2001 it was still sold in excess of $80. This was a P/E of 66 based on trailing basic earnings per share of $1.22 for 2000.

By August 2001 the stock price had fallen to below $40. Even after the earnings and stock equity revisions were announced on October 16 and 17, the stock still sold for $20 (as late as October 23).

By November 30, the stock price was $0.26 per share and on 15 January 2002, the stock was suspended from trading on the New York Stock Exchange.

The Indictment

The Grand Jury indictment of Skilling and Lay included the following (p. 3, Section 5).

> 5. As detailed below, defendants KENNETH L. LAY ("LAY"), JEFFREY K. SKILLING ("SKILLING"), and their conspirators, engaged in a wide-ranging scheme to deceive the investing public, including Enron's shareholders, the SEC, and others (use "Victims"), about the true performance of Enron's businesses by: (a) manipulating Enron's publicly reported financial results; and (b) making public statements and representations about Enron's financial performance and results that were false and misleading in that they did not fairly and accurately reflect Enron's actual financial condition and performance, and they omitted to disclose facts necessary to make those statements and representations fair and accurate.

The indictment concluded that the conspiracy's objectives included (paragraph 17).

- Reporting recurring earnings that falsely appeared to grow smoothly by approximately 15 to 20 percent annually and thus create the illusion that Enron met or exceeded the published expectations of securities analysts forecasting Enron's reported earnings-per-share and other results;
- Touting falsely the success of Enron's business units;
- Concealing large losses, "write-downs," and other negative information concerning its business units;
- Masking the true magnitude of debt and other obligations required to keep the company's varied and often unsuccessful business ventures afloat;
- Deceiving credit rating agencies in order to maintain an investment-grade credit rating; and
- Artificially inflating the share price of Enron's stock, including attempting to stem the decline of Enron's share price in 2001.

If true, these are bad actions, but none of the above, by themselves, are likely to cause the bankruptcy of a healthy corporation. But Enron was to a large extent a trading corporation, and the bad press in the fall of 2001 led to the loss of its trading partners and financing.

Conclusions

This book will investigate the factors leading to Enron's collapse and try to separate out the significant from the less significant. We shall see that there were real factors contributing to the collapse and that there were intangibles that eroded the market's faith in Enron's accounting and business practices, and created the "run on the bank" that was described by Jeffrey Skilling (ex-CEO of Enron).

The objective of Chapters 2 and 3 is to establish that there were no sufficient reasons for a casual reader of Enron's published financial statements to conclude that this was a financially distressed corporation. Chapter 4 starts the explanation of the fall.

The book will also review elements of the 2006 Skilling–Lay trial. The objective is not to determine the innocence or guilt of the two men. Rather, it is to dissect the accusations and testimony so that some of the fluff can be cast aside, and it can be better determined whether the Skilling–Lay trial was fair or not. The two men should not have been convicted because investors lost money when Enron collapsed, but the bankruptcy of Enron looms large as a primary factor in their convictions. At least there is reason to think that the Judge and the US Attorneys thought it was very important.

The position of this book's author is that Enron (Skilling and Lay) could have presented more and better financial information to the public. But the US Attorneys also distorted the facts and arguments during the Skilling–Lay 2006 trial at a level that was comparable to the accounting distortions of Enron. The US Attorneys "knew" Skilling and Lay were guilty and used strategies to gain convictions, given their guilt.

It is interesting to note that four of the most significant events leading to Enron's bankruptcy did not give rise to immediate accounting entries. These events were (1) hiring of Fastow; (2) departure of Kinder and Wing from Enron; (3) giving of Marks a relatively free hand to make international investments; (4) shift of mark to marketing accounting.

Reference

McLean, B and P Elkind (2003). *The Smartest Guys in the Room: The Amazing Rise and Scandalous Fall of Enron*. New York, NY: Portfolio (the Penguin Group).

Chapter 2

Enron as of 31 December 2000*

Assume financial analysts were limited to using the year 2000 annual report of Enron to evaluate the financial affairs of the company. Of course, financial analysts should use information beyond the publicly available financial information if they can legally obtain it. In this chapter we analyze Enron's likelihood of bankruptcy using only its year 2000 annual report.

At what stage should the security analysts have recognized that things were not well with Enron? Let us review the year 2000 annual report of Enron. First consider the net incomes and earnings on common stock for the years 1998–2000.

Year	Earnings on common stock*	Net income*
1998	686 million	703 million
1999	827	893
2000	896	979

*p. 31 of the annual report.

---

*All page references in this chapter are to Enron's year 2000 annual report or to the Skilling–Lay trial proceedings unless otherwise indicated.

Both the $896 and $979 million earnings for the year 2000 are after a $326 million charge to reflect the decrease in the value of the Azurix investment. In addition, there is a $39 million gain on The New Power Company (TNPC) stock. This gain on the TNPC investment will be important in later discussions because Enron has taken inappropriate steps to protect that gain.

Enron reported that it earned a total of $2409 million on common stock from 1998 to 2000, with the earnings increasing each year. There were reasons for its stock price to become "high" (but not as high as it went). A reader of the annual report may readily conclude that the Enron stock price was too high without concluding that Enron was heading toward bankruptcy.

Azurix

The $326 million write down of the Azurix investment reported in the annual report is important for several reasons. First, it reflected a bad investment (or a badly run investment) of Enron. In July 1998, Enron purchased Wessex Water Company for an amount equal to $1.9 billion to $2.2 billion, approximately a 28% premium over the Wessex stock price. This purchase premium was difficult to recover given the unfriendly regulatory climate in England (Wessex was a small English water and sewage company). Second, the accounting for Azurix figured significantly in the Skilling–Lay trial.

Reberra Mark, who had been in charge of Enron's international trust, was in charge of Azurix. The goal was to use Wessex as a base to launch a worldwide water distribution and water treatment company. In addition to the company in England, Azurix operated in Mexico, Canada, and Argentina. Each acquisition was purchased at premium prices reflecting Mark's optimism that the water business represented large profitable business opportunities. Thus at the very instant of acquisition, the water assets were recorded at costs materially larger than their expected fair values. (The costs were the prices paid for the assets.) Mark's hope was that the assets were worth more than the fair value to Enron.

While the purchase of these assets at inflated prices might have been managed badly and reflected bad business judgments, there was no criminal intent in their purchase and initial accounting (as any observer would agree).

For more details of Enron's attempts to form a worldwide water business, see Fox (2003) or McLean and Elkind (2003).

The Trial

Ms Ruemmler states (p. 17694):

> Mr. Lay and Mr. Skilling had been unable to sell $10 billion or so in international assets that were dragging the company down. Mr. Skilling had estimated that those assets were worth only about half of what they were being carried on Enron's books for. An expensive venture into Enron's — into the water business — you heard about this — Azurix was just a colossal disaster.

Remember that the water business was acquired by Mark, Skilling, and Lay at premium prices in 1998–1999. Azurix went public in 1999 at $19 a share. Skilling was not a supporter of Mark's efforts to build an international water empire. His valuation of the acquired assets was likely to be conservative.

It is not surprising that Enron management was not willing to concede defeat two years later. But Ms Ruemmler sees the refusal to write the assets down differently (p. 17820):

> They could not afford to take the $700 million Wessex goodwill loss that they needed to take, so they had to come up with a scheme to avoid that.
>
> The most powerful motive in the world to come up with a scheme to defraud Arthur Andersen is if you know that if you take a bigger loss, that it's going to mean certain death for the company because a credit downgrade will ensue.

But in 2000, Azurix was written down by $326 million. Maybe additional write-downs were needed, but remember this same management team paid a 28% premium over market value for Wessex to start with. It is not unusual for the current management of a firm to be reluctant to admit that they made a mistake in the amount paid for assets.

On 26 March 2002, the *New York Times* reported that Enron sold Wessex Water Company to YTL Corporation, a Malaysian company, for $777 million cash. There was pressure on Enron (and Azurix) to convert the Wessex asset into cash; so, this was a "fire sale".

Cash Flows

Since management can manipulate earnings, we must also consider cash flows for the three years.

	Net cash provided by operating activities*
1998	1640 million
1999	1228 million
2000	4779 million

*p. 34 of the annual report.

There are at least two cash flow items that could be adjusted. First, $1838 million "Proceeds from sales" of merchant assets and investments for 2000 (it was $2127 million in 1999). Since this amount for the year 2000 could be determined by the management's decisions to sell assets, one might want to adjust cash flow expectations for the future.

Second, the amount of deposits by the California customers was not explicitly given on p. 34, but to the extent it was included in "Net Cash Provided by Operating Activities" for the year 2000, it should be excluded since it is more like a loan than a cash flow generated from operations. The deposits of the year 2000 were expected to be repaid by Enron in 2001.

Using the above figures, the cash flow stream to investors for the three years seems to be healthy. In each of the three years 1998–2000, Enron paid an increasing amount of dividends, perhaps projecting the management's optimism.

	Cash dividends
1998	414 million
1999	467 million
2000	523 million

Operating Segments

Enron was divided into five business segments, including an Exploration and Production unit for oil and gas discovery and production. Of the five segments, all were profitable (earnings before interest, minority interests, and income taxes) except for the start-up Broadband Services that lost $60 million in 2000. Corporate and others (which included Azurix and Enron Renewable Energy Corp.) resulted in a $615 million deduction from income.

A buyer of Enron stock was not likely to be buying the stock because of incomes from Broadband or Azurix. But these two units were major parts of the Government's case against Skilling. Skilling is accused of having said good things about Broadband and Azurix, but the facts that there were losses associated with Broadband and Azurix were available to the investors.

One of the major deficiencies of Enron's reporting is that the different types of incomes were not adequately revealed. For example, we would like to know, how much of the income was related to the holding of Enron stock (and Enron stock price increases) by non-consolidated subsidiaries? How much was the result of price changes of Enron's merchant assets? How much was related to transactions involving financial securities and derivatives? It was not enough for the users of the report to be given the income by operating segments.

Other Income

Enron's equity in the earnings of the firm's unconsolidated equity investments was $87 million in 2000 (p. 31).

There is a $121 million "Gains on the issuance of stock by TNPC, Inc." that is not well defined. It is likely to be the result of either the sale in the market of part of the Enron investment in TNPC or a change in the market value of Enron's investment. More information regarding this $121 million gain would have been useful.

Lines of Credit

On 31 December 2000, Enron had current assets of $30.4 billion and current liabilities of $28.4 billion (net working capital of $2 billion). In addition, Enron had $4.2 billion lines of credit of which only $290 million was outstanding (p. 27).

> Certain of the credit agreements contain prefunding covenants.
>
> Management believes that the sources of funding described above are sufficient to meet short- and long-term liquidity needs not met by cash flows from operations.

We shall find that clauses allowing potential creditors to abrogate the credit agreements and the prefunding covenants will contribute to Enron's downfall. The extent of Enron's risk should have been better defined.

Return on Sales

It is interesting to inspect Enron's return on revenue for the three years.

	Year ended December 31* (dollars in millions)		
	2000	1999	1998
Total revenue	100,789	40,112	31,260
Income before interest, Minority interests, and Income taxes	2482	1995	1582
Income return on total revenue	0.025	0.050	0.051

*p. 31 of 2000 annual report.

The decrease in the return on total revenue could reflect a change in the product mix, a decrease in merchant asset gains, increasing competition, or some other factors. It is not a positive sign. The very large increase in revenue in 2000 was necessary for a relatively small increase in income.

Return on Equity

The returns on stock equity for the three years are as follows:

	Year ended December 31* (dollars in millions)		
	2000	1999	1998
Earnings on common stock	896	827	686
Total shareholders' equity	11,470	9570	7048
Return of stock equity	0.078	0.086	0.097

*p. 31 and 33 of the 2000 annual report.

The returns on stock equity for the three years are at best only fair. The average shareholder will not be very pleased with the firm earning a return on equity of less than 0.10. Enron's earnings performance for the three years was only mediocre given the $11 billion of stock equity investment at the end of the year 2000.

Capitalization

As of 31 December 2000, the reported long-term debt was $8550 million and total shareholders' equity (book) was $11,470 million. When the stock price was $80 a share, the firm's market value of stock was $60 billion. Long-term debt was 0.427 of the total accounting capital (long-term debt plus book equity). This is not a shockingly large percentage of long-term debt.

The definition of debt could be changed from long-term debt to total debt, and in addition debt revealed in footnotes could be included, but the fact is that Enron's capitalization was in reasonable shape based on the accounting reports as of December 2000. All the rating agencies rated Enron's unsecured debt as being in investment grade. The annual report correctly states, "Enron's continued investment grade status is critical to the success of its wholesale businesses as well as its ability to maintain adequate liquidity" (p. 27). Of course, the above debt measures leave out the debt of Enron's unconsolidated subsidiaries.

Note that the following note makes reference to the early settlement of debt and to the issuance of additional shares of Enron stock, but the magnitude of the debt and the amount of potential issuance are not disclosed (p. 27):

> Enron is a party to certain financial contracts which contain provisions for early settlement in the event of a significant market price decline in which Enron's common stock falls below certain levels (prices ranging from $28.20 to $55.00 per share) or if the credit ratings for Enron's unsecured, senior long-term debt obligations fall below investment grade. The impact of this early settlement could include the issuance of additional shares of Enron common stock.

While the above reference to stock issuance is of concern since it could adversely affect Enron's share price, it could not by itself cause bankruptcy. If accelerated debt repayment was linked to stock price or the firm's bond rating, this could cause bankruptcy.

In February 2001, Enron issued $1.25 billion zero coupon convertible senior notes (maturity value of $1.9 billion) that mature in 2021. The initial conversion premium was 0.45. This will not turn out to be a good investment for the buyers of the bonds. The large conversion premium highlights how good the financial health of Enron seemed to investors who based their opinion on the publicly available information. Since they expected the stock price to increase, they were willing to buy a convertible note with a large conversion premium.

Financial Risk Management

Enron's discussion of its risk management practices takes up more than a page of its annual report. The firm uses "a variety of financial instruments, including financial futures, swaps, and options" (p. 27).

Enron managed the following risks:

Commodity price risk;

Interest rate risk;

Foreign currency exchange rate risk;

Equity risk.

We shall see that the management of equity risk is most challenging (p. 28).

> Equity Risk. Equity risk arises from Enron's participation in investments. Enron generally manages this risk by hedging specific investments using futures, forwards, swaps and options.

Enron applied J. P. Morgan's RiskMetrics^{TM} approach. The failure of Enron does not reflect on the Morgan approach but rather the impossibility of removing all risks from a corporation's operations (p. 28) and Enron's ineffective hedging actions.

> The use of value at risk models allows management to aggregate risks across the company, compare risk on a

consistent basis and identify the drivers of risk. Because of the inherent limitations to value at risk, including the use of delta/gamma approximations to value options, subjectivity in the choice of liquidation period and reliance on historical data to calibrate the models.

This sophisticated description of the risk models did not apply to all Enron's hedges. Enron should have revealed that many of its hedges of investments were partial hedges (the hedge counterparty had very limited resources) that would not be effective for large value charges of the underlying assets or the value of Enron's stock.

The Audit

Arthur Andersen was Enron's auditor. The report of the independent public accountant included the conventional (standard) statement (p. 30):

> In our opinion, the financial statements referred to above present fairly, in all material respects, the financial position of Enron Corp. and subsidiaries as of December 31 2000 and 1999, and the results of their operations, cash flows and changes in shareholders' equity for each of the three years in the period ended December 31 2000, in conformity with accounting principles generally accepted in the United States.

Arthur Andersen was not charged with any crimes in connection with the audit leading to these financial statements.

The Balance Sheet

The firm's total assets were $65.5 billion. There were $5.3 billion of "Investments in and advances to unconsolidated equity affiliates". Natural gas transmission assets were $6.9 billion, and electric generation and distribution assets were $4.8 billion. It is important to note that Enron had real assets and had real operations as well as less real trading operations (wholesale business).

There were $904 million of "Company-obligated preferred securities of subsidiaries". There are cleverly structured preferred stock securities that give rise to an interest deduction for tax purposes, even though they are called preferred stock. This type of securities is not unique to Enron. It is a form of security that Wall Street Investment Banks like to sell and the issuance of which the US Treasury would like to prevent (but so far the Treasury has not been successful). This type of security is named Monthly Interest Preferred Stock (MIPS).

Mark-to-Market

Enron uses mark-to-market accounting for the instruments utilized in trading activities (p. 36). Unfortunately, mark-to-market accounting was also used in cases where the market value had to be estimated rather than observed. This practice introduced an excessive amount of arbitrary and subjective evaluations into the income and asset measures.

> Financial instruments are also utilized for non-trading purposes to hedge the impact of market fluctuations on assets, liabilities, production and other contractual commitments.

Securitizations

Enron sells interests in some of its financial assets. One type of sale transaction involves securitization. The securitization might take the form of a swap (p. 38). Gains on swaps in 2000 were $381 million and the proceeds were $2379 million. These transactions were of a material size.

Unfortunately, the footnote (3) and p. 38 do not supply adequate explanation for us to reach definite conclusions. For example, the swaps limit the risks assumed by the purchaser. Does this mean that the risk remains with Enron despite the "sale"?

There were $545 million of sales to Whitewing Associates. Enron recognized no gain or loss on these transactions (p. 42). Page 42 gives an amount of sales of $632 million. Whitewing has relevance in other aspects since it is an entity with ties to Enron employees.

In addition to selling financial assets, Enron also purchased $1.2 billion of equity interests in 2000.

Guarantees

> Guarantees of liabilities of unconsolidated entities and residual value guarantees have no carrying value and fair values which are not readily determinable… (p. 39).

Generally accepted accounting principles do not require the recording of a liability for guarantees. This is unfortunate since a guarantee by a corporation creates a liability for that corporation, and Enron had a significant number of guarantees.

Merchant Activities

The total value of Enron's merchant activities for the year ending on 31 December 2000 was $690 million, down from $1273 million at the end of 1999. The merchant investments were carried at fair value. The decrease in value was probably related to both decreases in value and sale of assets. Pre-tax gains from sales in 2000 were of $104 million and cash proceeds were of $1838 million.

Substantive merchant investments were made in energy, energy-intensive industries, technology-related power plants, and natural gas transportation (p. 40). Enron's efforts to hedge the gains on these investments led to accounting errors that contributed significantly to its bankruptcy.

Income Taxes

The 2000 annual report showed that the total Federal income tax as currently payable for 2000 was $112 million up from $29 million in 1999 and $30 million in 1998. Obviously, these are low tax bills for a profitable firm. The firm has had very large depreciation, depletion, and amortization deductions for taxes. A *New York Times* news article (17 January 2002) reported that in four of the last five full years, Enron actually paid zero Federal income taxes. Subsidiaries located in tax havens facilitated this tax strategy. Another factor was that the gains on merchant assets were not realized (for tax purposes); thus Enron did not have to pay tax on a large percentage of its accounting income (which included these unrealized gains). Stock options that are taxed to its executives give rise to a tax deduction for Enron. Enron also used a preferred stock structure so that the dividends on this stock resulted in a tax deduction as if the financing were debt.

The numbers in the annual report for tax expense will mislead a reader who wants to determine the actual amount of federal income taxes paid by Enron.

The firm has a $254 million alternative minimum tax credit carryforward. Will it ever be able to use this credit? It also has large tax loss carryforwards (p. 40).

Unconsolidated Equity Affiliates

The book value of unconsolidated equity affiliates was $5.3 billion. For the ten unconsolidated firms listed (p. 42), the voting interest was equal to or less than 50% and was 34% or larger.

The total owners' equity of these firms was $13.6 billion (Enron owned 0.39 of the equity). The long-term debt of these firms was $9.7 billion. Enron's proportionate amount of this debt was $3.8 billion. This is 0.42 of Enron's equity investment, and recognizing both the debt and equity in Enron's balance sheet (not required under accounting rules) would not change the firm's debt–capital ratio materially.

> In 2000, The New Power Company sold warrants convertible into common stock of The New Power Company for $50 million to the Related Party (described in Note 16)" (p. 43).

This transaction is more complex than that implied by the above or below "innocent" statements.

From time to time, Enron has entered into various administrative service, management, construction, supply and operating agreements with its unconsolidated equity affiliates. Enron's management believes that its existing agreements and transactions are reasonable compared to those which could have been obtained from third parties (pp. 42–43).

We will study the "unconsolidated equity affiliates" in forthcoming chapters since they contribute in significant ways to Enron's collapse.

Azurix (p. 43)

A related party subsidiary of Enron acquired an interest in Azurix. If the debt obligations of the related party are defaulted or if Enron's credit rating falls below specified levels, then Enron's convertible preferred stock will be sold to retire such debt. "The number of common shares issuable upon conversion is based on future common stock prices". A decrease in Enron common stock price could result in an enormous amount of dilution in the Enron stock value per share.

Unfortunately, the above paragraph is not as clear as a reader might like. The above is extracted from footnote 10 (p. 43) and the footnote leaves us with many questions. How much preferred stock can be issued, and convertible on what basis?

Derivatives (p. 44)

At December 31 2000, Enron had derivative instruments (excluding amounts disclosed in Note 10) on 54.8 million shares of Enron common stock, of which approximately 12 million shares are with JEDI and 22.5 million are with related parties (see Note 16), at an average price of $67.92 per share on which Enron was a fixed price payor.

Again there is too much not revealed. To what type of derivatives does the above note refer? If Enron was a fixed price payer what does it receive?

Pension and Other Benefits (pp. 45–46)

> Enron maintains a retirement plan (the Enron Plan) which
> is a noncontributory defined benefit plan covering sub-
> stantially all employees in the United States and certain
> employees in foreign countries. The benefit accrual is in
> the form of a cash balance of 5% of annual base pay.

On 31 December 2000, the fair value of plan assets was $858
million for pension benefits. The benefits obligation at the end of the
year was $746 million. Unfortunately, the asset total included plan
assets of the firm's ESOP of $116 million. Assuming zero value for
the ESOP, the plan assets would be $858 - 116 = 742 million.

While not in great shape, the pension fund assets and liabilities are
reasonably close in value.

For the other benefits the firm offers, there are only $64 million
assets to cover $124 million of obligations.

Related Party Transactions (pp. 48–49)

The existence but not the extent of related party transactions was
disclosed.

> In 2000 and 1999, Enron entered into transactions with
> limited partnerships (the Related Party) whose general
> partner's managing member is a senior officer of Enron.
> The limited partners of the Related Party are unrelated to
> Enron. Management believes that the terms of the trans-
> actions with the Related Party were reasonable compared
> to those which could have been negotiated with unrelated
> third parties.

The "hedging" of Enron's merchant investments is a significant contributor to Enron's collapse. In 2000, Enron entered into
derivative transactions with the entities with a combined notational
amount of approximately $2.1 billion to hedge certain merchant
investments and other assets. Enron's notes receivable balance was

reduced by $36 million as a result of the premium owed on derivative transactions. Enron recognized revenues of approximately $500 million related to the subsequent change in the market value of these derivatives, which offset market value changes of certain merchant investments and price risk management activities. In addition, Enron recognized $44.5 million and $14.1 million of interest income and interest expense, respectively, on the notes receivable from and payable to the Merchant Investment Entities.

The following note is the trigger of a $1.2 billion reduction in Enron's stock equity in 2001.

> In 2000, Enron entered into transactions with the Related Party to hedge certain merchant investments and other assets. As part of the transactions, Enron (i) contributed to newly-formed entities (the Entities) assets valued at approximately $1.2 billion, including $150 million in Enron notes payable, 3.7 million restricted shares of outstanding Enron common stock and the right to receive up to 18.0 million shares of outstanding Enron common stock in March 2003 (subject to certain conditions) and (ii) transferred to the Entities assets valued at approximately $309 million including a $50 million note payable and an investment in an entity that indirectly holds warrants convertible into common stock of an Enron equity method investee. In return, Enron received economic interests in the Entities $309 million in notes receivable, of which $259 million is recorded at Enron's carryover basis of zero, and a special distribution from the Entities in the form of $1.2 billion in notes receivable, subject to changes in the principal for amounts payable by Enron in connection with the execution of additional derivative instruments.

Again, the notes are not quite as clear as we would like but they do disclose much relevant information.

Another note indicates that Enron "contributed" a put option. Does this mean it "sold" or was the put option a "gift"? In any event the put option contributed to a $36 million loss to Enron (p. 49).

Also, Enron contributed a put option to a trust in which the Related Party and Whitewing hold equity and debt interests. On 31 December 2000, the fair value of the put option resulted in a $36 million loss to Enron.

There was an internal Arthur Andersen communication in February 2001 that "suggests that Andersen may have had concerns about the disclosures of the related-party transactions in the financial statement footnotes. Andersen did not express such concerns to the Board" (p. 203 of the Powers Report).

Conclusions

The Enron Annual Report for 2000 supplies a large amount of financial information. Several footnotes could have been written in a more informative manner, but a reader should have been alerted to the fact that more information was needed.

On the other hand, Enron had a reasonable operating performance in 2000 (as well as 1999 and 1998) and its balance sheet appeared to be strong. Including the debt of the unconsolidated subsidiaries does not change that conclusion if the debt and the equity ownership of the subsidiaries are shown in proportionate amounts.

The Special Purpose Entities (SPEs) of Enron are a separate issue. A careful (thorough) analyst of Enron would like to know more about the SPEs.

There is very little in the 2000 annual report that leads a reader to conclude that financial distress will occur within the next 12 months. There are many signs that the Enron common stock did not deserve to be sold in the $80s, but that is different from concluding that the firm was in financial distress.

In Chapter 5, we will find that many of the numbers relied on in this chapter need to be adjusted. Given the need for revision, Burton

Malkiel faults the accounting statements (*The Wall Street Journal*, 16 January 2002):

> The bankruptcy of Enron — at one time the seventh largest company in the US — has underscored the need to reassess not only the adequacy of our financial reporting systems but also the public watchdog mission of the accounting industry, Wall Street security analysts, and corporate boards of directors.

He recommends self-regulation:

> And, in the end, we need to create a powerful and effective self-regulatory organization with credible disciplinary authority to enforce accounting rules and standards. It would be far better for the industry to respond itself to the current crises than to await the likelihood that the political process will do so for them.

Senator Fred Thompson made a very perceptive observation (*Newsweek*, 4 February 2002, p. 17):

> The real scandal here may not be what's illegal, but what's permissible.

It would have been very useful if the year 2000 Enron Annual Report had discussed in detail the sources for the incomes for the years 1998–2000.

The failures of Enron's accounting were more a failure to execute the spirit of the current accounting standards, than it was that the standards did not exist. Also, rather than attempting to inform the reader of all relevant financial information, if there was a way to keep information from the reader, too often Enron followed that way. Thus, a minimum of information regarding the SPEs of Enron was presented to the reader of its annual report. But the long-term debt of these entities ($9.7 billion) was given in the report, if not in Enron's balance sheet.

References

Fox, L (2003). *Enron: The Rise and Fall*. Hoboken, NJ: John Wiley & Sons, Inc.

McLean, B and P Elkind (2003), *The Smartest Guys in the Room*. New York, NY: Portfolio (the Penguin Group).

Chapter 2 — Case
Enron (2000) Annual Report

There follows relevant pages of Enron's year 2000 annual report.

a. Identify the hints that there might be financial trouble despite the reasonable earnings record.
b. As a bank-lending officer, using only the information contained in the annual report, would you authorize a loan of $500,000,000 to Enron?
c. Did you note any sections that were not as clear as you would like?

Chapter 3

First Six Months of 2001: Before the Storm*

Enron's reported earnings on common stock were $788 million for the first 6 months of 2001 (compared to $58 million for 2000). For the quarter ending 30 June 2001, earnings were $383 million (compared to $268 million for 2000). Up to 30 June 2001, Enron was doing well based on the published financial statements.

The long-term debt was $9355 million as of 30 June 2001, up from $8530 million as of 31 December 2000. The stockholder equity was $11,740 million, up from $11,470.

The cash flow from operating activities was a negative $1337 million for the 6 months ending 30 June 2001. The primary item causing the negative cash flow was $2342 million use of cash for net margin deposit activity (this was the repayment of loans). Excluding net margin deposit activity, cash provided by operations was a positive $1005 (p. 31).

Capital expenditures were $1200 million up from $1009. Equity investments were $1088 million up from $390 million. These were bullish indicators.

The dividends paid were $256 million down from $265 million. This reflects the changes in the amount of outstanding preferred and common shares, and is not significant.

---

*All the page references in this chapter are to the 10Q of 14 August 2001 or the Skilling–Lay trial proceedings unless otherwise indicated.

The repurchase of common stock was $209 million compared to $129 million for the first 6 months of 2000. The increase in shares repurchased might be mistakenly interpreted to be a slight bullish signal. It is more likely to be the repurchase of shares from the management.

Net cash paid for income taxes was $167 million in the first six months of 2001 and $33 million for 2000. This reflects an increase in taxable income.

In March 2001, Enron paid $330 million for 39 million shares of Azurix common stock. Increasing its ownership of Azurix implies that the initial investment was thought to be desirable and Enron was increasing its investment in that subsidiary. This transaction in 2001 was important since during the Skilling–Lay trial the Government would argue that both Skilling and Lay knew that the Azurix investment was overvalued. For example, the closing argument of Ms K. H. Ruemmler quotes Ben Glisan (p. 17818), the Enron Treasurer:

> And third, we knew that as a result of Raptor, but also other areas, inclusive of Broadband and Azurix, that there were charges that should be taken. So the request that was made of me by Mr. Whalley and Lay was "How much could we take without losing our credit rating?"

The point being made seemed to be that more of the Azurix investment should be written off as an expense. But an additional investment in Azurix was made in March 2001 because it is estimated that the net present value of the benefits exceeded the cost of the new investment. Enron management was bullish on Azurix. Maybe they were incorrect, but being incorrect is not a crime.

Ms Ruemmler gives a reason for not taking a goodwill loss (p. 17820):

> A final decision has been made that we are not willing to take any goodwill impairment on Wessex.
> Who made that final decision? Mr. Lay made it. How do you know? You know it because Mr. Glisan told you

that they had a discussion that they couldn't take any more than a billion dollars. They could not afford to take the $700 million Wessex goodwill loss that they needed to take, so they had to come up with a scheme to avoid that.

The most powerful motive in the world to come up with a scheme to defraud Arthur Andersen is if you know that if you take a bigger loss, that it's going to mean certain death for the company because a credit downgrade will ensue.

She states (p. 17820), "that there was a $1 billion value problem, potential loss, in Azurix". But a potential loss is not a valid reason for writing down an asset or to accuse a manager of a crime because the write-down was not made. Any accounting value of an asset is a potential loss.

Continuing (p. 17821), Ms Ruemmler goes on:

One, did Enron tell AA that there was a water growth strategy to avoid a goodwill impairment?

Of course, a firm does not need growth to avoid a goodwill impairment. This line of irrelevant argument goes on for several pages. Sean Berkowitz (US Attorney), in his closing argument, also makes the point that Enron did not have a growth strategy. He does not argue that Azurix and Wessex (an asset of Azurix) did not have value (p. 18297).

The way that they avoided a goodwill write-down in the third quarter was by lying to Arthur Andersen. There's no question, no question, ladies and gentlemen, that Enron was telling Arthur Andersen that it had a growth strategy for Wessex. No question.

If Enron had a growth strategy for Azurix, it would not prove that the Azurix asset cost did not exceed its value (thus should be written down). Also, even if Enron did not have a growth strategy for Azurix, it would not prove that it should therefore be written down. In summary, the existence or lack of a growth strategy for Azurix was not an indication of the value of the asset's cash flows compared to the asset's cost.

In March 2001, Enron acquired the limited partner's equity on the unconsolidated equity affiliate Joint Energy Development Investments Limited Partnership (JEDI) for $35 million. This acquisition leads to JEDI now having to be consolidated (later we shall learn that JEDI should have been consolidated since 1997). JEDI owns an investment of 12 million shares of Enron common stock valued at $785 million and other assets of $670 million. JEDI had debts of $950 million of which $620 million was third-party debt and $330 million was owed to Enron. Chapter 7 explores JEDI in more detail.

Dabhol Power Company

Enron owns 65% of the economic interest in Dabhol Power Company (India) which owns a 740 MW power plant and was expanding the plant to a 2184 MW power capacity and was building a LNG regasification facility in conjunction with the power plant. General Electric and Bechtal Corporation each owned 10%. Dabhol's customer, the Maharastra state utility owned 15%.

The debt of Dabhol is non-recourse to Enron (Enron is not liable for Dabhol's debt).

There was a dispute between the Dabhol investors and various Indian authorities (the Electricity Board, the state government, and the federal government of India). "As a result of these disputes, the 740 MW power plant is not being dispatched.... Further, Dabhol has suspended construction activity on Phase II" (p. 10). There is a major disagreement about the amount that should be paid to Enron and its fellow capital contributors. The buyer of the electricity claimed that it was being overcharged. The outlook for Enron's Indian investment is not sanguine, but it is not hopeless.

Despite those difficulties "Enron does not believe that any contract dispute related to Dabhol will have a material adverse impact on Enron's financial condition or results of operations". This is a very naïve conclusion. Enron has almost a $2 billion investment in India at risk. The total cost of the plant exceeded $2.9 billion.

On 21 May 2001, *The New York Times* on page 1 had a heading "Electricity Crisis Hobbles an India Eager to Ascend". The article stressed the economic advances made by India but pointed out that "an electricity crisis represents one of the major hurdles to India's ability to hoist itself into the front ranks of the global economy". The Dabhol Power Company may belatedly turn out to be a sensible investment.

Business Segment Information

For the 6 months ending 30 June 2001, the following incomes were reported by segment:

	Income (loss) before interest, minority interests, and income taxes
Wholesale services	$1557 million
Retail energy services	$100 million
Broadband services	$(137) million
Transportation and distribution	$335 million

Note that a large loss for Broadband ($137 million) was reported. The Government will argue that excessively optimistic reports were given relative to Broadband.

Except for Broadband, all the business segments reported profitable operations. Wholesale services and retail energy services had improved results compared to year 2000.

The Trial: Broadband

Enron's 10Q report of 14 August 2001 showed a loss for Broadband services of $137 million. Ms Ruemmler focuses on

Skilling's statements rather than the reported results of operations (p. 17742):

> For the benefit of the stock, Mr. Skilling lied about the revenues of the business, and Mr. Skilling failed to fully disclose the business failure to the public.

And later she states (p. 17746):

> They're trying to leave the impression that this business is succeeding. It's gaining traction. It's actually going to be profitable in the future. No question it was a startup, no questions they were only going to be posting losses; but they needed to show that they were generating some revenue.

In order to limit Broadband's reported loss, a decision is made to cut expenses (p. 17748):

> At this meeting, there's a decision made to drastically cut expenses, to reduce head count, because they have to protect the number that has been given to The Street, the $65 million loss number.
>
> The agreement coming out of that meeting, Mr. Rice and Mr. Hannon told you, was to keep the loss target at $65 million and to drastically cut costs.

Ms Ruemmler could have added that reducing expenses may be a reasonable way of reducing an expected loss. Instead, the opportunity is taken to imply that lies are being told to misstate the amount of loss. Maybe lies were told but it should not be implied that cost reduction implies the existence of a crime. Also, a $137 million Broadband Services loss was reported for the six months ending 30 June 2001.

Derivatives

"Derivative contracts are entered into with counterparties who are equivalent to investment grade" (p. 14). This statement is important since the failure of Enron to maintain an investment grade rating accelerated its slide down the slope to bankruptcy.

Related Party Transactions

A senior officer of Enron (Andrew Fastow) was the general partner of the related party partnerships. He sold all his financial interests in the related parties as of 31 July 2001, and after that date he no longer had any management responsibilities for these entities. The partnerships were no longer related to Enron. But the damage had been done.

"All transactions with these partnerships (the Partnerships) have been approved by Enron's senior risk officers as well as reviewed annually by the Board of Directors" (p. 15). It is not obvious that this statement is exactly true. We shall review this later in more detail.

In 2000, Enron committed to deliver to a related party 12 million shares of Enron common stock in 2005. Enron "entered into derivative instruments" (p. 15) "that eliminated the contingent nature of existing restricted forward contracts executed in 2000". Since the report does not define the nature of the derivative instruments, we cannot analyze the nature and function of these transactions.

In exchange for its common stock Enron received $827.6 million of notes receivable. If the related party is not "independent" of Enron the $827.6 million should not be recorded as an asset by Enron and there should not be an increase in stock equity.

Real Volumes

It is not easy to forget that Enron was a real corporation dealing with real things. For example, Enron's sales of gas were 24,554 billion of British thermal units in the first 6 months of 2000 and increased to 34,427 in 2001 (p. 25). Crude oil and liquids sales increased by 51% is the period 2000–2001. Total electricity volumes increased by 110% (p. 25).

The revenues from retail energy services increased from $734 million in 2000 to $1250 million in 2001. Income before interest, minority interests, and taxes, increased by 92% (p. 26).

Financial Condition

> Management anticipates cash from operating activities in the second half of 2001 to be positively impacted by

reduced working capital requirements and overall operating activities (p 31).

Return on Revenue

The revenues for the first six months of 2001 were $100,189 million and income before interest, minority interests, and income taxes, was $1588 million. The return per dollar of revenue was $\frac{1588}{100,189} = 0.016$, down from 0.025 for the year 2000. It was becoming more difficult for Enron to make profits from a dollar of revenue.

Return on Equity

The earnings on common stock for the first six months of 2001 were $788 million and the shareholders' equity was $11,740 million. The return on stock equity was $\frac{788}{11,740} = 0.067$ for 6 months or a 0.134 equivalent return for the year. This was better than the returns earned for 1998–2000, but it is not a great return.

Conclusions

Enron's 10Q of 14 August 2001 submitted to the SEC is a collection of good news. Based on published information, Enron had excellent performance in the first six months of 2001, and its financial condition was healthy.

Jeffrey Skilling claims that he resigned as CEO in August 2001 when the financial situation of Enron was good. If all he did was read the 10Q submitted on 14 August 2001, he had reason to be sanguine.

The Editorial of the 18 January 2002 issue of *The Wall Street Journal* includes the following:

> The culture wanted to believe in Enron's promises, which helps explain why 16 of 17 Wall Street analysts rated Enron a "buy" as recently as last October.

The Senate Governmental Affairs Committee found that 10 of 15 security analysts reporting on Enron rated the stock as a "buy" or a "strong buy" as of 8 November 2001. Rather than concluding that the recommendations were based on the low Enron stock price, Senator Joseph Lieberman attributed the bad investment advice (*ex post*) to a conflict of interests (the selling of investment banking services):

> No matter what the market does, analysts just seem to keep saying "buy" (*Wall Street Journal*, 28 February 2002, p. A1).

We can add that the published financial statement (filed on 14 August 2001) reported reasonable operating results for the first 6 months of 2001. In evaluating decisions that were made prior to 16 October 2001 we should be careful to consider only the information that was available to the public during that time period.

Would different accounting standards and practices have led to a different bankruptcy date for Enron? Different accounting practices would have affected the timing of its bankruptcy. Its stock price is likely to have declined at an earlier date since the reported incomes would have been much reduced. The panic might have started earlier.

With less opaque accounting and fewer accounting errors it is possible that Enron would not have entered bankruptcy. But its stock price would not have reached the peaks it reached in 2000. If Enron had followed different accounting practices (less optimistic), the gains made by investors prior to August 2001 would have been less and if the accounting incomes during 1998–2001 had been lowered, some of the losses would have been suffered by other investors. But losses would have taken place. When a stock is too high, someone has to lose.

The Government claims that Skilling and Lay lied about Enron's financial health before 1 July 2001, and that there were signs of weakness (e.g., Broadband and Enron Energy Services). But neither Skilling nor Lay acted on this information by selling the majority of their stockholdings and it is more likely that they believed that Enron was a healthy corporation from a financial viewpoint.

Chapter 3 — Case

There follows extracts from the Enron 10Q dated 14 August 2001 for the quarterly period ended 30 June 2001 (pp. 2–36).

Things to note:

1. Losses from Broadband — $137 million (p. 12).
2. Related party transactions (p. 15).
3. Earnings of $788 million for 6 months; Earnings of $383 million for quarter ending 30 June 2001.
4. Nothing that raises significant concerns.

Chapter 4

Sherron Watkins' Letter to Kenneth L. Lay

Jeffrey K. Skilling unexpectedly resigned from his CEO position on 14 August 2001 after a little over six months on the job. Kenneth L. Lay resumed his chores as CEO. Shortly after this, Lay, the chairman and CEO of the Enron Corporation received an unsigned letter. The author of this letter was later identified to be Sherron S. Watkins, a vice president for Corporate Development at Enron, when she sent an expanded signed letter to Lay and offered to speak with him to describe her concerns.

Mrs Watkins deserves credit for disclosing to Lay that a huge accounting–finance problem existed at Enron. The fact that not every statement in the letter can be verified or understood is less important than the overall tone of the letter and the urgent request for action. Consider the first paragraph:

> Has Enron become a risky place to work? For those of us who didn't get rich over the last few years, can we afford to stay?

In the second paragraph she identifies accounting issues:

> Enron has been very aggressive in its accounting — most notably the Raptor transactions and the Condor vehicle. We do have valuation issues with our international assets and possibly some of our EES MTM positions.

But aside from identifying "aggressiveness" and "valuation issues" she does not adequately enlighten Lay as to what exactly is wrong in a language that he can understand. In fact, in the next paragraph she states "the valuation issues can be fixed...". She does not see an easy fix to Raptor and Condor, and she does not clearly explain the problem other than the fact "we will have to pony up Enron stock". She gives no indication of the magnitude of the dilution. While she could have expanded on the specific accounting problems, it is clear that the problems she describes should be investigated.

The next paragraph of the letter identifies $800 million from merchant asset sales to "a vehicle (Condor) that we capitalized with a promise of Enron stock in later years". Mrs Watkins asks "Is that really funds flow or is it cash from equity issuance?" It is possible that it is a sale of assets by Enron to itself. But Lay could not conclude that the $800 million asset sale is really equity issuance based on this letter.

She then cites over $550 million of fair value gains on "stocks via our swaps with Raptor". The nature of the swaps is not explained. We know merchant assets increased in value (the gains were recognized), and then decreased in value. The losses were not recognized in a timely fashion. This could have been explained more clearly to Lay. But Arthur Andersen had approved the accounting for these losses.

Mrs Watkins is very accurate in forecasting accounting scandals:

> I am incredibly nervous that we will implode in a wave of accounting scandals. My eight years of Enron work history will be worth nothing on my resume, the business world will consider the past successes as nothing but an elaborate accounting hoax.

She asks that Lay and Richard Causey (chief accounting officer) study the accounting problems.

She describes Raptor as being capitalized with LJM equity but then Raptor paid a cash fee to LJM that effectively eliminated LJM's investment in Raptor. LJM effectively had zero equity investment in

Raptor. She then states:

> The majority of the capitalization of the Raptor entities is
> some form of Enron N/P, restricted stock and stock rights.

But rather than "capitalization" she probably means assets of Raptor. At a minimum the meaning is cloudy.

> Enron entered into several equity derivative transactions
> with the Raptor entities locking in our values for various
> equity investments we hold.

I suspect this wording could be improved. There was an attempt by Enron to lock in its values for various equity investments, and she was correct; the attempt was flawed.

She properly voices concern; about the adequacy of the footnotes to the financial statements.

> My concern is that the footnotes don't adequately explain
> the transactions. If adequately explained, the investor
> would know that the "entities" described in our related
> party footnote are thinly capitalized, the equity holders
> have no skin in the game, and all the value in the enti-
> ties comes from the underlying value of the derivatives
> (unfortunately in this case, a big loss) AND Enron stock
> and N/P.

She states that if the stock gains had been hedged with independent firms "substantial premiums" would have to have been paid.

> In other words, the $500 million in revenue in 2000 would
> have been much lower. How much lower?

I suspect she means there would have been costs of buying puts (or the equivalent) that would have reduced the income of 2000. However, real puts would also have reduced the losses that were incurred when the stock prices fell. She never clearly states that the hedges in place with the Raptors were not effective (valid) for large price changes.

She offers two courses of action and suggests that Lay choose one:

1. The probability of discovery is low enough and the estimated damage too great; therefore we find a way to quietly and quickly reverse, unwind, write down these positions/transactions.
2. The probability of discovery is too great, the estimated damages to the company too great; therefore, we must quantify, develop damage containment plans and disclose.

There was actually only one appropriate course of action "quickly reverse, unwind, write down these positive transactions", and in addition "quantify, develop damage containment plans and disclose". Choosing only one of the above two courses of action was likely to be wrong.

The Two Gains

Mrs Watkins raises the issue regarding the $500 million related party transaction, "the related party entity has lost $500 million in its equity derivative transactions with Enron". Secondly, she questions a $800 million fund flow resulting from merchant asset sales to Condor (a SPE). She does not clarify whether the $800 million affected Enron's income.

But, *The New York Times* (17 January 2002) carried a news item with the banner "Enron Letter Suggests $1.3 Billion More Down the Drain". This is a stretch relative to Watkins' letter since she did not suggest that $1.3 billion more was lost.

It is reasonable to want more information regarding the above two transactions. For example, if Enron reported a $500 million gain that equaled the amount the related party lost, and if the related party was unable to pay the $500 million, then Enron would be overstating its income by $500 million.

The effect of the $800 million funds from merchant asset sales to Condor on Enron's income ranges from zero to $800 million depending on the magnitude of the gain Enron recorded and whether any or all of the gain was a valid gain. Certainly, an estimate of $1.3 billion over- statement of income is an extreme estimate for these two transactions.

Actions by Lay

Lay gave a copy of the letter to James V. Derrick, Jr., Enron's General Counsel" (p. 173 of the Powers Report). Derrick and Lay decided that an outside law firm, Vinson & Elkins (V & E) should conduct an investigation. Their charge was to determine whether the facts cited by Watkins "warranted further independent legal or accounting review" (p. 173).

V & E reported in writing the results of its investigation on 15 October 2001. They concluded that the preliminary investigation did not warrant a "further investigation by independent counsel or auditors" though the Raptor transactions created "a serious risk of adverse publicity and litigation" (p. 176). As the Powers Report states regarding the V & E investigation, "The scope and process of the investigation appears to have been structured with less skepticism than was needed to see through these particularly complex transactions" (p. 177). The actions of Lay regarding Watkins' letter appear to have been reasonable at the time. With the aid of hindsight, more might have been done. Certainly, V & E should have been more thorough in its investigation of the allegations made in the letter. But Watkins' letter was probably too late to save Enron from bankruptcy.

The Trial

Ms Ruemmler (US Attorney) makes the point in the Lay–Skilling trial that Lay was not telling the truth regarding the Watkins letter (p. 17802).

> What did Mr. Lay say about this anonymous letter in his trial testimony? He said that he didn't receive this anonymous letter.

Given that Lay had given Watkins' letter to James V. Derrick, Enron's General Counsel, and they both decided to give the letter to Enron's outside law firm (Vinson & Elkins) and all this was in the Powers Report (p. 173), Lay was not testifying that he did not receive Watkins' letter, but rather that he did not receive an ill-defined "anonymous letter". Watkins' letter was not anonymous long enough to be described by a US Attorney as being anonymous in the Skilling–Lay trial. It is not right for a US Attorney to imply that Lay was not telling the truth when he denied under oath receiving anonymous letter, but did readily admit to receiving Watkins' letter. When I read Ms Ruemmler's closing arguments (p. 17802) regarding Watkins' letter I was initially confused when she spoke of the anonymous letter. It was clever of Ms Ruemmler to question Lay about the anonymous letter when she could have clarified her question by referring to Watkins' letter. It was clever, but not a right thing to do.

Later (p. 17805) Ms Ruemmler states "I submit to you that Mr. Lay made that statement that there was no shoe to fall, that the investigation into Ms. Watkins' allegations was predetermined". Does Ms Ruemmler mean that the law firm Vinson & Elkins did not submit an honest unbiased evaluation of Watkins' letter? If she does not mean that, then what does she mean by "predetermined"?

Sean Berkowitz (US Attorney) continues on this same path (p. 18286) in the Government's rebuttal arguments:

> The Watkins' letter is devastating... And so he predetermined what was going to happen with the Watkins' investigation. No other shoes to drop? How did he know, ladies and gentlemen? He didn't, and that's a lie. And it was a lie to keep the stock price up. And that's count 1 and it's honest services. And you can convict him on this statement.

But Lay was basing his conclusion on the Vinson & Elkins report. It might be a bad judgment, but it is not a crime to base a statement on a report from a highly respected law firm. Lay's statements were truthful compared to the way the US Attorneys twisted his comments so that they could be labeled lies.

Lay's e-Mail and Stock Transactions

On August 20, Mr Lay exercised options on 25,000 shares at an exercise price of $20.78 (an investment of $519,500). Some of the stock was sold back to Enron to repay loans to buy stock.

Earl J. Silbert, Lay's lawyer said that Lay's sale of stock in 2001 was to pay loans that financed his investments that had declined in value (*The New York Times*, 21 January 2002, p. 1). Lay had put up Enron shares as collateral for his other investments. As the value of both the investments and the Enron stock decreased he had to supply cash to the lenders. He got the cash by selling his Enron stock to Enron.

Lay had purchased technology stocks, and in 2001 these stocks had tanked. One company whose stock Lay had purchased was The New Power Company (TNPC). Enron also had made a major investment in TNPC (see Raptor III). Not only did TNPC fall to less than $1 per share, but Lay's investment also was inappropriate, given Enron's large investment in TNPC.

On 21 August 2001, Lay sent an e-mail to Enron employees that expressed his optimism regarding Enron and its stock price. He exercised options on 68,620 shares to buy at $21.56 (an investment of $1,479,000).

On 26 September 2001, Lay again sent an e-mail to Enron employees that expressed his confidence in the company and its stock.

The First Doubters

In the spring of 2001, Bethany McLean wrote the article "Is Enron over-priced?" for Fortune Magazine and was an early doubter of Enron as a common stock investment. Her main question regarding Enron was how it was earning its profits. She wrote that Enron's financial report was not clear on that issue (*The New York Times*, 28 January 2003, p. All).

While Miss McLean was right to question Enron's stock price (in the high $80s) she did not anticipate its financial distress in her writings.

Chung Wu of Paine Webber's Houston office sent a message to clients early on 21 August warning that Enron's "financial situation is deteriorating" (*The New York Times*, 27 March 2002, p. 11). An Enron employee objected to Wu's negative observations. Mr Wu was fired a couple of hours later.

On the same day, Paine Webber sent out a message retracting Mr Wu's statements.

We do not know the basis of Mr Wu's recommendation. Paine Webber explained his firing as resulting from his not following company policies.

Mr Wu was able to obtain a position with a competitive brokerage firm.

Daniel Scotto of BNP Paribas recommended in August 2001 that Enron securities should be classified as "neutral" rather than "buy". Shortly after this he was placed on family leave. BNP Paribas denied that the leave was linked to the investment advice (see *The Wall Street Journal*, 29 January 2002, p. C1).

The Trial

On 15 March 2006, Sherron S. Watkins testified in the Skilling–Lay trial. She is famous for her warning in August 2001 that Enron could "implode in a wave of accounting scandals". She testified that her warnings were not taken seriously.

That is not accurate. Lay met with Watkins and discussed her concerns. He then asked Vinson & Elkins (Enron's lead law firm) to investigate. The law firm concluded that there was no substance behind Watkins' letter. Also, if one reads the letter one can find concerns and warnings but one cannot find evidence of a crime by Lay.

Conclusions

Mrs Watkins' August letter did a terrific job of identifying the fact that Enron had problems with its accounting practices. She identified SPEs (Raptors and Condor) and transactions for which questionable accounting practices were used or where there was inadequate disclosure. She did less well describing exactly what were the accounting problems. One cannot read (or study) her letter and talk with confidence about the exact nature of Enron's accounting problems. Of course, she wrote the letter expecting that the reader was somewhat familiar with the basic facts. Lay would likely not have been enlightened by the letter in terms of specific actions that should have been taken. On the other hand, a careful investigation of the transactions identified by Watkins might have advanced the dates of discovery from October and November to August and September. It will only be in October that an independent observer starts to learn the details of Enron's accounting and financial problems. Would advancing the date of discovery and having Lay define the issues have saved Enron or merely advanced the date of its demise? It would have changed the names of some of the victims.

Ms Ruemmler focuses on the information flowing to Lay in August (p. 17694):

> Mr Lay is repeatedly informed about more and more bad news. Sherron Watkins warns the company could implode in a wave of accounting scandals.

Lay gives the letter to the firm's law office (V & E) and asks for a report. Where is the crime?

Chapter 4 — Case

There follows extracts from Mrs Watkins' letter of 14 August. This letter was not signed. A subsequent letter was signed.

> *Has Enron become a risky place to work? For those of us who didn't get rich over the last few years, can we afford to stay?*
>
> *Skilling's abrupt departure will raise suspicions of accounting improprieties and valuation issues. Enron has been very aggressive in its accounting — most notably the Raptor transactions and the Condor vehicle. We do have*

valuation issues with our international assets and possibly some of our EES MTM positions.

The spotlight will be on us, the market just can't accept that Skilling is leaving his dream job. I think that the valuation issues can be fixed and reported with other good will write-downs to occur in 2002. How do we fix the Raptor and Condor deals? They unwind in 2002 and 2003, we will have to pony up Enron stock and that won't go unnoticed.

To the layman on the street, it will look like we recognized funds flow of $800 million from merchant asset sales in 1999 by selling to a vehicle (Condor) that we capitalized with a promise of Enron stock in later years. Is that really funds flow or is it cash from equity issuance?

We have recognized over $550 million of fair value gains on stocks via our swaps with Raptor. Much of that stock has declined significantly – Avici by 98 percent from $178 million, to $5 million; the New Power Company by 80 percent from $40 a share, to $6 a share. The value in the swaps won't be there for Raptor, so once again Enron will issue stock to offset these losses. Raptor is an LJM entity. It sure looks to the layman on the street that we are hiding losses in a related company and will compensate that company with Enron stock in the future.

I am incredibly nervous that we will implode in a wave of accounting scandals. My eight years of Enron work history will be worth nothing on my resume, the business world will consider the past successes as nothing but an elaborate accounting hoax. Skilling is resigning now for 'personal reasons' but I would think he wasn't having fun, looked down the road and knew this stuff was unfixable and would rather abandon ship now than resign in shame in two years....

The complete letter is six times as long as the above excerpt.

Chapter 5

The Clouds Burst*

On 16 October 2001 Enron reported a loss of $664 million for the third quarter of 2001 and Enron announced that it was taking a $544 million deduction (after-tax) from earnings of past years. The $544 million charge was related to losses suffered on investments in The New Power Company, investments in Broadband activities, and stock investments in other high-tech companies. This $544 million deduction was related to transactions of years 1997–2000 with the LJM2 partnerships created and managed by Andrew Fastow. In addition to the $544 million charge, on 17 October 2001, Enron announced that it was reducing its stock equity by an additional $1.2 billion. Enron's common stock price immediately fell and there were decreases in Enron's credit rating to BBB — and BAA3 the lowest level of investment grade debt with warnings that further downgrades were possible (likely?). To retain its trading partners and ability to raise short-term capital to finance its trading operation, Enron needed investment grade credit ratings. On 22 October 2001, the Securities and Exchange Commission started to investigate Enron's financial affairs.

On 21 October 2001, Andrew S. Fastow resigned (or was forced out) from the CFO position of Enron. He was placed on leave. On 31 October, the SEC announced it was conducting a formal investigation on Enron's financial affairs.

---

*All the page references in this chapter are to Enron's 8-K of 8 November 2001 or the Skilling–Lay trial proceedings.

By 28 November 2001, Enron's stock price had fallen to $.51 per share. Dynergy withdrawing its 9 November 2001 offer to buy Enron for about $9 billion accelerated the fall.

The form 8-K filed by Enron on 8 November 2001 reported the restatement of the financial statements to record the $1.2 billion reduction to shareholders' equity, and various income statement and balance sheet restatements. The 8-K expanded on Enron's news releases of 16 and 17 October 2001 and revealed an additional $413 million of income deductions related to Chewco transactions and $103 million related to LJM1 transactions.

The income restatements described in the 8-K resulted because three unconsolidated entities should have been consolidated from 1997 to 2001 to be in accordance with the generally accepted accounting principles. The incomes reported for the years 1997–2000, and the first six months of 2001 could not be used with reliability since they had to be revised. Two of the entities (Chewco and JEDI) should have been consolidated since 1997 and the third (LJM1) should have been consolidated since 1999 because of inadequate independent capitalization. In order not to be consolidated, each special purpose entity (SPE) was required to have at least 3% of its assets financed with independent equities.

The $1.2 Billion Reduction to Stock Equity

The $1.2 billion reduction to the stock equity was revealed in an October 16 news release and in the firm's 8-K report filed with the SEC on 8 November 2001. This specific adjustment did not affect Enron's liquidity or its earnings record. It merely reversed a journal entry to a receivable and to stock equity that should not have been recorded following generally accepted accounting principles. The stock equity account should not be increased when the asset received is a risky receivable.

The $1.2 billion adjustment was split between the year 2000 ($372 million) and 2001 ($828 million). While there may have been some financial analysts who focused on the amount of accounting book value, it is unlikely that the stock equity restatement was a material factor moving Enron to bankruptcy, except for the fact that the accounting adjustment reduced faith in the firm's accounting reliability.

Enron originally reported total stock equity of $11,740 million as of 31 December 2000. The restated equity for that date was $10,306 million. Debt was increased from $10,229 million to $10,857 million restated. Again, while it is upsetting that adjustments were necessary, the magnitude of the reductions in stock equity was not sufficiently large enough to cause financial distress directly. The adjustments to the past incomes were more significant.

The Relevance

The recordings of the $1.2 billion notes receivable and the $1.2 billion increase in stock equity in 2000 and 2001 were incorrect. Reversing the entries in November 2001 did not affect the real financial position of Enron. On the other hand, we can surmise that reducing the stock equity by $1.2 billion probably affected some conclusions relative to Enron's financial health, even though the firm's true financial health was not affected by the accounting entry.

Similarly, the adjustment of the net incomes for 1997 through 2001 did not change Enron's financial health as of November 2001. However, the perceptions of Enron's past profitability and thus the expectations of future profitability were changed materially. Most importantly, the market was very rapidly losing faith in the past accounting statements of Enron.

Adjustments to Net Income

The restatement of Enron's net incomes (8-K of 8 November 2001) (p. 4) is as follows:

	Net Income (millions)				
	1997	1998	1999	2000	Totals
As reported	105	703	893	979	2680
Restated	9	590	643	847	2089
Reductions	96	113	250	132	591

As of 8 November 2001, there was a reductions of $591 million in the earnings of 1997 through 2000, not the $544 million reported on October 16 (there were differences in classifications).

The fact that Enron made almost $3 billion of net income (restated) over the 4 years in question is impressive. While common stock investors would be misled by the original income measures, none of the above restatements would, by themselves, lead to a forecast of financial insolvency. In the year 2000 Enron made a restated income of $847 million. Even more importantly, it made $1134 million of recurring income in 2000. However, the fact that one set of accounting errors has been revealed naturally leads to a fear that additional surprises remain.

The measures of Recurring Net Income for the 4 years are impressive.

	1997	1998	1999	2000	Totals
Recurring Net Income (as reported)	515	698	957	1266	3436
Recurring Net Income (restated)	419	585	707	1134	2845
Reductions	96	113	250	132	591
Chewco and JEDI (reductions)	28	133	153	99	413

Most of the restatements (70%) were associated with Chewco and JEDI. LJM1 gave rise to $103 million of the reductions.

The above measures of reductions and restated incomes differ slightly from those shown on p. 3 of the Powers Report, which also differ from those shown on p. 42 of the Powers Report. All three sources show reductions in net income of between $400 and $600 million. The restated incomes for the 4 years, total in excess of $2 billion for all the sources.

The Special Committee

Enron's 8-K reported the fact that the Board of Directors elected Dean William Powers (of the University of Texas Law School) to the Board and appointed Dean Powers as Chairman of a Special Committee of the Board to conduct an investigation and review the transactions between Enron and related parties. We refer to this report as the Powers Report.

Related Party Transactions

Pages 7–15 of the 8-K of 8 November 2001 discussed in some detail the transactions that Enron conducted with related parties. These transactions will be discussed later in this book.

Further Adjustments

The primary concern regarding Enron's financial situation as of November 2001 is whether there are further accounting adjustments that will be necessary. Do the SPEs hold additional surprises? Are there losses associated with the SPEs that will require recognition and were some of the revenues already reported not justified following accepted accounting procedures? Given the magnitude of the adjustments to income ($591 million) already recognized in the November 2001 8-K report, it would not be surprising if there were additional adjustments.

14 November 2001

Lay sent a message to all Enron employees summarizing a conference call to give investors (security analysts) an overview of the company. He stated:

> In hindsight, we definitely made some very bad investments in our non-core businesses over the past several years. Those include investments in Azurix, India and

Brazil. They have performed far worse than we could have ever imagined when we made these investments. Because of these bad investments, we've become over-leveraged as a company. The negative impact of those investments was exacerbated through the extensive use of debt capital both on and off our balance sheet. We also entered into related party transactions that led to a loss of investor confidence, which has been very damaging. We've been criticized for our lack of transparency and our hard-to-understand financial and operating disclosures; and on top of it all, we discovered errors in our financial statements, as discussed in our 8-K filing last week, that required a restatement of previously reported earnings.

He expressed optimism regarding operations.

Our core businesses remain strong and consistent sources of significant earnings and cash flows for the company. I also remain optimistic that the actions we've taken over the past couple of weeks have addressed our customer and counterparty credit and liquidity concerns. According to our business unit leaders, we have definitely seen improvement in our counterparty relationships.

He was also optimistic regarding the investment grade credit ratings.

We continue to meet regularly with credit rating agencies and believe that our liquidity enhancements and scheduled asset sales will strengthen our balance sheet and maintain our investment grade credit rating.

The Triggers

On 5 May 2001, Enron's stock closed at below $59.78. This set off a trigger in Osprey Trust that required Enron to pay $2.4 billion to the investors in the Osprey Trust.

On 5 September 2001, Enron's stock closed at below $34.13. This set off a trigger in the Marlin Trust that required Enron to pay $915 million to debt investors in the Marlin Trust.

Another trigger was a change in bond rating to less than the investment grade. On 28 November 2001 the rating agencies lowered Enron's rating to below investment grade (The Enron stock price was below $4). The payments of a large amount of debt were accelerated. All of the above triggers played important roles in the Enron bankruptcy.

The Loyal Investors

Enron stock had its supporters even as its price fell. A prime example was Alfred Harrison of Alliance. During the fall of 2001 (after October 22) Alliance bought over $35 million of Enron stock (*The New York Times,* 3 March 2001, p. 11). *Ex post* we know that Alliance's investment strategy was a scandal. But remember, based on the revised financials (as of the mid-November, 2001), Enron was still a profitable firm. It was only after the bad press (and bad accounting) chased away the trading partners and lenders that the continuation of Enron's operations became impossible.

Lawrence White of New York University (*The New York Times,* 24 February 2002, p. 13) is critical of the bond rating agencies for having failed to anticipate Enron's collapse before November 2001.

> There was a group of independent analysts that should have been in a position to blow the whistle early about Enron's true condition: Moody's Investors Service, Standard & Poor's and Fitch ratings. Through their evaluation of a company's creditworthiness, the Big Three rating agencies provide investors with an important assessment of its financial health. In this case, their judgments were too little, too late.

To avoid this situation the rating agencies would have to move beyond relying on published financial information and talking with executives. They would have to demand information from the corporation's management. If they did not receive the information, the rating agencies should withhold opinions.

In the case of Enron, did the rating agencies know what questions to ask? It is difficult to say since with the aid of hindsight we can structure the questions that should have been asked, but would we be as wise without hindsight?

If information is being hidden from the public it is probably also being hidden from the rating agencies. The users of the ratings have to understand the limitations of the ratings.

The Trial

The US Attorneys found it difficult to admit that adverse news reports and short selling contributed to Enron's downfall. They seemed to think incorrectly that recognizing these facts would affect the extent of guilt or innocence of Skilling and Lay. Consider the following statement by Ms Ruemmler:

> But the idea that there was some secret conspiracy between the *Wall Street Journal* and the short- and short sellers and that secret conspiracy brought down the seventh largest corporation in the country is nonsensical. It's absurd. It's ridiculous. Don't buy it (p. 17698).

We agree with Ms Ruemmler that there was no secret conspiracy but that many of the articles (not only in the *Wall Street Journal*) and the selling of the stock (some of which were short sellers) drove down the stock price which helped confirm the fact that Enron was in financial difficulty.

> Again, the Defendants want you to focus on this short seller/*Wall Street Journal* conspiracy because it takes the focus off of them. It takes the focus off the lies that they told and the choices that they made. It's diversionary tactic (p. 17698).

Skilling and Lay could both be guilty of all counts (or innocent) and the news articles and stock selling could still have contributed to the collapse of Enron.

Mr Berkowitz followed the same path:

> The Defendants would have you believe that the reason that happened is the *Wall Street Journal* and short sellers and Andy Fastow. Every company in the country has negative articles written about it. Practically every company in the country has individuals who sell their stock short. Almost every company has people who steal from the till, ladies and gentlemen. They don't go bankrupt. That's not what drives a company into bankruptcy (p. 18244).

But not every company has an Andy Fastow. He was unique.

While Skilling and Lay were not on trial for causing Enron's bankruptcy, Mr Berkowitz did not want the jury to forget this unfortunate fact (p. 18243):

> And it led us to those two men, ladies and gentlemen. And that's why we're here today. Let's not forget that Enron went bankrupt when we're considering the credibility of these people, all right? This was the seventh largest company in the country, and it went bankrupt in a matter of months.

Conclusions

The 17 December 2001 Form 8-K submitted by the Enron Corporation to the SEC described the petitions for relief under Chapter 11 of the Bankruptcy Code. Thus one of the great American corporate success stories came to an untimely end. Many innocent people (employers, investors, etc.) were severely harmed by the demise of Enron. What were the causes of this debacle?

A close inspection of the 2000 Annual Report and the 10Q dated 14 October 2001 reveals little financial information that leads to a conclusion that bankruptcy is likely. The firm's stock equity was $11,740 million reported as of 30 June 2001 and $10,306 million as adjusted. For the 6 months ending 30 June 2001, Enron earned $829 million of Net Income and for the year 2000, it earned $847 million (adjusted numbers).

Beginning in 1997, Enron failed to consolidate two subsidiaries and one subsidiary in 1999 that in 2001 it agrees should have been consolidated. With consolidation $591 million of Enron's earnings resulting from transactions with previously not-consolidated entities had to be eliminated. But there still remains $2089 million of Net Income for the years 1997–2000 and $2845 of Recurring Net Income.

As a result of the 10Qs submitted in October and November 2001, Enron's stock price and credit rating were battered. A trading firm needs both access to credit and an investment grade credit rating, and Enron lost both of these credit facilities. Enron's operating results in the second half of the year 2001 suffered accordingly. The firm had major losses in the third and fourth quarters of the year 2001.

Obviously, while the reported incomes would mislead investors and it is disappointing that the restatements were necessary, by themselves, they do not move a disinterested party to conclude that just based on these events Enron should be seeking protection from creditors. Until the new reports forecasted doom, credit sources evaporated, and trading partners no longer were willing to trade with Enron, Enron was a profitable entity.

Thus, while it is disconcerting that accounting mistakes were made, the mistakes were not of the relative magnitude that normally leads to bankruptcy (at least based on available financial information as of 8 November 2001).

The bankruptcy resulted from the ripple effects of many news articles concerning Enron. These news articles contained some incomplete and misleading reporting. Lenders and trading partners were frightened by the threat of financial distress when the only thing likely to cause financial distress was the fear of financial distress.

Lessons to be learned: One, a trading firm relying on external capital cannot afford not to be transparent in its financial affairs. Secondly, if a large amount of debt is used to finance trading operations, an attempt should be made to use long-term debt so that the long-term debt and the stock equity provide an adequate buffer against lenders' panic.

It was not known financial facts that caused Enron's financial distress but rather the reporting of the financial events and accounting mistakes in a dramatic fashion that triggered a panic on the part of Enron's trading partners and creditors. In November 2001, the market did not accept the extent of uncertainty associated with the accounting information being supplied by Enron and its accountants.

When the financial analysts encountered items in Enron's financial reports that they did not understand, they should have insisted on explanations. Lacking explanations, the analysts should not have given an opinion on the company or if they gave an opinion it should have been clearly qualified (the limitations defined).

While Jeffrey Skilling (ex Enron CEO) had personal reasons for coming to the following conclusion, there is also an element of truth to the statement:

> It is my belief that Enron's failure was due to a classic run on the bank, a liquidity crisis spurred by a lack of confidence in the company. (*The Wall Street Journal*, 8 February 2002, p. A3.)

The *New York Times* (29 November 2001) also used this term "Collapse Evoking Memories of Old-Time Run on a Bank". There remains the issue of who (or what) caused the run.

Chapter 5 — Case

There follows extracts from the Enron 8-K dated 8 November 2001. In this filing Enron revealed that $1.2 billion reduction of shareholders' equity as well as a restatement of its financial statements of 1997 through 2000 because there were unconsolidated entities that should have been consolidated. The "Recurring Net Income Restated" for

1997–2001 still adds up to $2849 billion. No year has a negative income.

Aside from the upsetting fact of two accounting errors (both under-standable and forgivable) there is nothing that implies bankruptcy is imminent.

Chapter 6

The 100-Year Flood*

On 19 November 2001 Enron's 10-Q for the third quarter of 2001 was filed with the SEC. The firm reported a loss on common stock of $664 million (this was consistent with the 16 October 2001 news release). The $664 million loss included $768 million of reported investment losses.

A note contained the warning "the previously issued financial statements for these periods and the audit reports covering the year-end financial statement for 1997 though 2000 should not be relied upon." This is consistent with Enron's previously issued form 8-K of 8 November 2001 (see Chap. 5).

The SEC was investigating related party transactions, and Enron's Board of Directors formed a special committee to conduct an independent investigation (described in Chap. 5).

Liquidity Actions

To restore investor confidence Enron took several steps. It borrowed $3.0 billion from its lines of credit to provide immediate liquidity and borrowed $530 million from JP Morgan Chase and Citicorp. The Dynergy Corporation bought $1.5 billion of preferred stock of

---

*All the page references in this chapter are to the 10-Q of 19 November 2001 unless there is a specific reference to the Powers Report or the Skilling-Lay trial proceedings.

Northern National Gas Company (an Enron subsidiary). This was part of the Enron–Dynergy Merger agreement. Enron also anticipated $800 million in net proceeds from asset sales.

Enron initiated a plan for immediately restructuring its business. The new structure was described as (page 11 of Enron's 10-Q report of 19 November 2001):

> "Core businesses are the consistent franchise businesses for which Enron has a distinct competitive advantage. These businesses, collectively, generate significant earnings and cash flows. These businesses include:
>
> Gas and power businesses in North American and Europe;
> Coal businesses in North America;
> Retail businesses in North America and Europe; and
> Natural gas pipeline businesses.
>
> Non-Core businesses are businesses that do not provide value to Enron's core businesses. These primarily are part of Enron's global assets and broadband services segments. Enron has approximately $8 billion invested in these businesses and the return from these investments is below acceptable rates. Accordingly, Enron is developing a plan to exit these businesses in an orderly fashion".

Because of the downgrade in Enron's credit rating (a ratings event) a $690 million note-payable's date of payment was advanced to 27 November 2001 (p. 12). Other debts would be advanced if Enron lost its investment grade rating (p. 12):

> "In the event Enron were to lose its investment grade credit rating and Enron's stock price was below a specified price, a note trigger event would occur. This could require Enron to repay, refinance or cash collateralize additional facilities totaling $3.9 billion, which primarily consist of $2.4 billion of debt in Osprey Trust (Osprey) and $915 million of debt in Marlin Water Trust (Marlin). In the event such a trigger event occurs and Enron cannot timely

issue equity in an amount sufficient to repay the notes and restructure the obligations, Enron is obligated to pay the difference in cash".

The summary statement with respect to debt payment acceleration is

"An adverse outcome with respect to any of these matters would likely have a material adverse impact on Enron's ability to continue as a going concern".

The Dynergy Merger

The Dynergy Merger is discussed in some detail in the 10-Q, but, we know that Dynergy withdrew from the merger agreement and Enron fails to escape from its dire fate.

The Restatement

The financial activities of Chewco Investments, LP (Chewco), a related party SPE, should have been consolidated into Enron's financial statements beginning in November 1997. Chewco was an investor in Joint Energy Development Investment Limited Partnership (JEDI). JEDI was first consolidated in the first quarter of 2001 but should have been consolidated beginning in November 1997.

Also, LJM1 (the general partner's managing director was Andrew S Fastow) should have been consolidated beginning in 1999.

The effect of the accounting changes associated with consolidating these three subsidiaries was to reduce the reported incomes since 1997. For example, the net income for 1997 was reduced from $105 million to $26 million, for 1998 was reduced from $703 million to $564 million, and for 1999 from $893 million to $635 million (pp. 16–17). These measures are slightly different from those of the 8th November 2001, 8-K and from the Powers Report (see below).

The book equity measures were also restated, but the changes were relatively minor (a reduction of about 10% for the year 2000). Debt was increased by less than 10%.

There were also $1.2 billion of accounting errors made in the second quarter of 2000 and the first quarter of 2001 (p. 10). The result was an overstatement of notes receivable and stock equity. In 2001, it was recognized that the $1.2 billion of notes should have been subtracted from stock equity. Thus, the stock equity amounts reported on the unaudited balance sheets of Enron were overstated by approximately $1.2 billion on 31 March 2001 and 30 June 2001.

The Powers Report (p. 42) indicated the following adjustments needed to be made to the income (these measures differ from those of p. 3, *The Powers Report* and p. 4 of *Enron's 8-K* of 8th November 2001).

	Reported net income	Decrease in income
1997	$105 million	$28 million
1998	703 million	133 million
1999	893 million	153 million
2000	979 million	91 million
Total	2680 million	405 million

Enron's reported debt would be increased by $628 million in 2000 as a result of the consolidations.

The Triggers

If Enron lost its investment grade rating, note triggers would occur. The triggers could require immediate payment of debt. These provisions had two consequences. First, the threat of immediate debt repayment resulted in a heightened risk of bankruptcy. Second, the need of Enron to maintain investment grade rating allegedly led to crimes by Skilling and Lay.

For example, Ms Ruemmler states (p. 17820 of Skilling–Lay trial proceedings):

> "The most powerful motive in the world to come up with
> a scheme to defraud Arthur Andersen is if you know that

if you take a bigger loss, that it's going to mean certain death for the company's because a credit downgrade will ensue".

Mr Berkowitz also made a similar point (p. 18297 of Skilling–Law trial proceedings):

> "Mr. Glisan tells you that Mr. Whalley and Mr. Lay said, 'How much can we take and still keep our credit rating?' 'How much can we take?' Reverse engineering. Mr. Glisan said, 'A billion dollars.' That's what they took. They had more that they didn't take, and the way that they got through that, ladies and gentlemen, was by lying to Arthur Andersen".

There is no question that Skilling and Lay would want Enron to maintain an investment grade. Loss of investment grade would result in the end of Enron's trading activities. But that does not mean, by itself, that they intend to commit crimes in order to maintain investment grade. Also, even the Government claims Skilling and Lay were trying to help Enron avoid financial disaster by retaining its investment grade bond rating.

Conclusions

The loss of $664 million for the third quarter of 2001 announced on 16 October 2001, the announcement of a $1.2 billion reduction in stock equity, and the reduction of the net incomes of 1997, 1998, 1999, and 2000 all contributed to a feeding frenzy of news articles questioning Enron's accounting practices and equally importantly its financial manipulations. From 16 October 2001 to the bankruptcy announcement on 2 December 2001 the news reports regarding Enron were unrelentingly negative. They did not improve after 2nd December. All the errors that had been made by Enron were magnified by the press, and this led to the firm's December bankruptcy.

Chapter 6 — Case

Enron's 10-Q report dated 19 November 2001 for the quarterly period ended 30 September 2001 was effectively Enron's death knell. It was 83 pages long, but nothing in it leads one to forecast Enron's end.

The report revealed a $664 million loss for the quarter (the loss was first reported by Enron on 16 October 2001). While Enron's debt still had an investment grade rating the future was not sanguine.

There follows a brief extract from the 10-Q dated 19 November 2001.

Chapter 7

JEDI and Chewco: Not the Movie*

JEDI was initially a $500 million unconsolidated subsidiary owned jointly by Enron and CALPERS (California Public Employees' Retirement System). It was formed in 1993. Since Enron and CALPERS had joint control of JEDI, Enron did not consolidate JEDI into its consolidated financial statements. This meant that JEDI's debt was revealed in a footnote but not on Enron's balance sheet. Also, a proportionate amount of JEDI's gains and losses were included in Enron's income statement. The total JEDI income appeared in a footnote to Enron's annual reports.

In November 1997, Enron wanted to redeem CALPERS' ownership interest in JEDI for specific and justifiable business reasons. CALPERS was willing to be bought out. Enron purchased CALPERS' 50% interest in JEDI for $383 million. It needed to resell the interest before the end of the year (1997) otherwise it would have to consolidate JEDI with its financial affairs. This would adversely affect both Enron's debt and reported income.

Fastow identified Michael Kopper, an Enron employee as the person who would together with Fastow form a SPE (special purpose entity) called Chewco to purchase CALPERS' ownership in JEDI then owned by Enron. Fastow helped Kopper to organize and finance

---

*All the page references in this chapter are to the Powers Report unless otherwise indicated.

Chewco. They failed to get permission from the Enron Board for Kopper to participate as a manager or investor in Chewco.

To help it buy CALPERS' interest in JEDI for $383 million, Chewco borrowed $240 million from Barclays bank. The debt was guaranteed by Enron (Chewco paid Enron a fee).

Chewco also borrowed $11.4 million from Big River Funding (controlled by Little River Funding, which was owned by SONR#2 which was owned by William Dodson, a close friend of Michael Kopper). Little River borrowed $331 thousand from Barclays and gave $341 thousand to Big River, which gave $11.4 million to Chewco.

Chewco also received a $132 million advance from JEDI. Thus to finance the purchase of CALPERS' interest in Jedi, we have

Barclay (direct loan)	$240.0 million
Big River (equity)	11.4*
SONR #1	0.115**
JEDI (advance)	132.00
Total	$383.515 million

*$10,000 from William Dodson
**$1000 from Michael Kopper and $114,000 from M. Kopper and W. Dodson

The $11.4 million from Big River consisted of $11.1 million received directly from Barclays Bank, and 0.3 million from Little River constituted the equity investment.

This Enron annual report (2000) states "an officer of Enron has invested in the limited partner of JEDI and from time to time acts as agent on behalf of the limited partner's management". Thus, the conflict of interest was clearly revealed. The officer referred to in the previous quotation was either Kopper or Fastow.

To understand the implications of what happens next, it helps to understand some arcane accounting rules.

SPEs

Enron like many corporations used SPEs to raise capital and to manage risk. If the SPE had the right characteristics it was not consolidated with Enron's financial statements. Not consolidating kept the SPE's debt off Enron's balance sheet.

To obtain guidance as to whether or not to consolidate a SPE we go to EITF Abstracts, Issue No. 97-6 (Emerging Issues Task Force Abstracts of 16 November 2000). We find the following statement very confusing:

> The Task Force reached a consensus that the transition requirements of Issue 96-20 should be changed to apply to a qualifying SPE that either (1) holds only financial assets it obtained in transfers that were accounted for under the provisions of Statement 125 or (2) has substantive capital investments by a third party, as required by Issue No. 90–15,... (Note: This consensus was nullified by Statement 140. See STATUS section) ... (p. 933).

Status

> Statement 125 was issued in June 1996. Statement 125 was replaced by Statement 140 in September 2000. Statement 140 nullifies the consensus reached in this issue.
>
> Paragraph 25 of Statement 140 permits a former qualifying SPE that fails to meet one or more conditions for being a qualifying SPE to be considered a qualifying SPE under Statement 140 if it maintains its qualifying status under previous accounting standards, does not issue new beneficial interests after the effective date, and does not receive assets it was not committed to receive before the effective date.

The above quotations are included in order to emphasize the lack of clarity regarding the accounting for SPEs. Practice (the SEC) allowed a SPE not to be consolidated if:

1. An independent investor owned equity equal to 3% or more of the SPE's total assets. This equity interest must be maintained during the entire period of non-consolidation.
2. The independent investor exercised control over the SPE.

There were many accountants who were not familiar with the 3% requirement of the SEC. The logic of this rule is not obvious.

Given the SEC rule, why is it important that the 3% equity must be owned by independent investors who exercise control over the SPE? Assume a SPE owns a large amount of Enron stock and the stock goes up. If Enron owns some of the SPE's equity, Enron can report the proportionate amount of increase in stock value as income. If the SPE were consolidated, there would be no increase in income because Enron's stock went up.

The independent equity investor must exercise control in order for there to be no consolidation. But Enron organizes the SPE to do some function on behalf of Enron. It has to control the SPE's activities sufficiently so that the desired function is achieved.

To require that, the independent exercise control destroys the basic objective of organizing the SPE. In the year 2001, the requirements for a SPE not to be consolidated laid the foundation for misuse by Enron.

The Use of Special Purpose Entities (SPEs)

Enron established special purpose entities for five primary purposes:

1. To finance assets and keep the debt off the balance sheet.
2. To create the so-called accounting hedges.
3. To sell assets to the SPE and thus be able to realize gains on those assets.
4. To sell to the SPE Enron assets that will have losses in the future.
5. To control and limit risk.

To use a SPE to finance assets and to keep the debt off the balance sheet were widely used and accepted practices. The use of a SPE also limits the risk to the parent corporation and may be useful as a type of organization that leads to efficiencies by facilitating joint ventures.

The appropriateness of using the SPEs to create the so-called accounting hedges depends on the extent economic hedges are also created so that there really is an effective hedge. Each case would have to be evaluated individually.

To use a SPE to buy a firm's assets so that gains may be realized and reported as income, ranges from being a marginally appropriate action to being misleading and inappropriate. Assume the parent wants to sell an asset. The first alternative is to sell it to a third party. If a third party buyer cannot be found, the buying by a SPE may be the only alternative for a rapid sale. As stated above, this is "marginally appropriate" since it is not going to be obvious that the transaction was arms length, and thus the gain can appropriately be realized. If the sale takes place before the end of an accounting period and the parent buys back the asset after the new accounting period begins, it is likely that there was not really a sale, and the gain on sales should not have been recognized.

Using a SPE to buy assets that may have future losses, requires a large amount of cooperation between the SPE and the parent. Since the SPE may have losses, the parent must compensate the SPE, if the SPE is acting in a rational manner. The likely reason for the parent to sell assets that may lose value to a SPE is to keep the losses off the parent's income statement. But if the SPE will be compensated for those losses, then the parent would really suffer losses despite having sold the asset. Thus with good accounting, very little (or nothing) would be achieved by a parent selling a risky asset to a SPE to avoid reporting losses. This type of transaction stretches one's imagination. It would have to be accomplished using faulty accounting (that did not note the parent's obligation for losses) or with the SPE accepting a risky investment with no compensation.

In order for a SPE's financial affairs not to be consolidated with the financial affairs of the parent, it is necessary that the SPE has 3% of independent equity which exercises control over the SPE. This 3%

is of the SPE's total assets and must be maintained during the entire period of nonconsolidation. Further, the parent cannot control the SPE. If there is no 3% independent equity, the financial affairs must be consolidated. In Enron's case (Chewco) one equity contributor (Barclays Bank) required that $6.6 million of cash be set aside by the SPE to protect its equity investment. This action effectively reduced the amount of independent equity below 3% with devastating financial consequences to Enron.

The use of SPEs is widespread among corporations. Nonconsolidating SPEs with 3% of independent equity where the parent does not control the SPE is in accordance with the generally accepted accounting practices which were in effect during 1997–2001.

Most of the SPE's capital will be debt (up to 97%). Since this could be a very large amount of debt, the SPE normally finds it easier to raise the debt capital if the parent guarantees the debt. The presence of these guarantees is revealed in the parent's financial reports in the footnotes, but the amount does not appear on the parent's balance sheet (this omission is very difficult to defend but may be consistent with the generally accepted accounting).

It was not the existence of the SPEs of Enron or the amount of the assets of the SPEs (and the debt guaranteed by Enron) that contributed to Enron's collapse, but rather the contributing factors were the faulty accounting for the affairs of the SPEs and the nature of the functions the SPEs were organized to perform. These functions were frequently marginal at best relative to their appropriateness.

For example, when used to create "Accounting hedges" the existence of the SPEs led Enron and Arthur Andersen to conclude that Enron's merchant assets were hedged when they were not effectively hedged economically for large price changes.

The situation with Enron's SPEs was complicated by the "related party issue". Enron's more controversial SPEs were organized by Enron's CFO (Andrew Fastow), and he was a major investor in these SPEs. Other Enron employees also invested in them. This created a conflict of interest's environment that required saintly behavior by these employees who were SPE investors to avoid the appearance of self-interest affecting the transactions between Enron and these SPEs.

Secondly, in order for a SPE not to be consolidated, it was necessary for the SPE not to be controlled by Enron (or Enron's management). Since an Enron manager was both a manager and an investor in Chewco, there was no independence, and the SPE should have been consolidated.

The Equity of Chewco

Assume Chewco's total assets in 1997 was worth $383 million. The 3% independent equity requirement required that $11.49 million of equity be present. Barclay invested $11.4 million in the SPE's equity and Kopper and Dodson $115,000 and the equity requirement seemed to be satisfied. Chewco and JEDI were not consolidated.

A complexity was revealed in the year 2001. In 1997, Barclay insisted that $6.6 million of Chewco's cash be set aside in a "reserve account" that was to be used to safeguard Barclay's equity investment. Effectively, Barclay's equity investment was reduced by $6.6 million.

Since there was not 3% independent equity investment, the SPE (Chewco) had to be consolidated in all the years after 1997. Arthur Andersen claims that it was not informed of the modified status of Chewco. We do not know if Enron was aware of the failure to keep Chewco independent. With the consolidation of Chewco, JEDI also had to be consolidated from 1997 to 2001.

JEDI

JEDI was a merchant investment fund and its assets were adjusted to fair value. Enron used the equity method of accounting for JEDI's income (a proportionate amount of JEDI's income was reported as Enron income).

JEDI owned 12 million shares of Enron stock. As the Enron share price went up, a proportion of the appreciation in the value of this stock was recorded by Enron as income. This practice ended in the third quarter of 2000 when Arthur Andersen decided that Enron recording income from an investment in Enron stock was not in accordance with generally accepted accounting principles since JEDI should have been consolidated.

Now we need to explain more accounting theory.

Gains and Losses from Stock Investment

Assume an independent entity buys 1,000,000 shares of Enron stock at a price of $50 per share and the price increases to $80. The independent entity has made an unrealized gain of $30 per share or $30,000,000 in total. Following mark-to-market accounting this gain will affect the independent entity's income. Enron's income will not be affected.

Now assume an entity, completely owned and controlled by Enron, buys 1,000,000 shares of Enron at a price of $50. When Enron did this sort of transaction, it would sometimes accept a notes receivable in exchange for the stock. Good accounting would require that there be no increase in stock equity or assets of Enron when the asset received is a note receivable. For this example, assume the entity paid $50,000,000 cash to Enron for the stock.

Now assume the stock price goes up to $80 per share. When the entity buying the stock was independent of Enron, there was a $30,000,000 gain. Now generally accepted accounting requires that there be no gain or loss for Enron associated with transactions involving Enron stock.

Consider the following table:

	Enron	An owned and controlled subsidiary
Assets	50,000,000	50,000,000 (Enron stock)
Stock equity	50,000,000	50,000,000

If we consolidate the financial affairs of the two entities we have:

	Consolidated
Assets	50,000,000
Stock equity	50,000,000

Now assume time passes and the controlled entity (and Enron) earns $20,000,000 and the value per share increases. The controlled entity is not marked-to-market. We now have:

	Enron	An owned and controlled subsidiary
Assets	70,000,000	70,000,000
Stock equity	70,000,000	70,000,000

If we consolidate the financial affairs we have

	Consolidated
Assets	70,000,000
Stock equity	70,000,000

But assume the controlled entity uses mark-to-market accounting and the value of its asset (Enron stock) increase to $80,000,000. The parent (Enron) should not record the $10,000,000 of market appreciation (above the $20,000,000 of earnings) as income. It results from the stock price change of Enron stock and this should not affect Enron's income.

The $30,000,000 increase in the Enron stock price does not give rise to Enron income or an increase in Enron assets. The $20,000,000 of Enron earnings are recorded.

In summary, if the controlled SPE is consolidated, then the change in value of the Enron stock owned by the SPE clearly does not affect the Enron income. If the SPE is not consolidated, the effect on Enron's income can be debated (but the author prefers there not to be an effect).

Since JEDI was not consolidated (incorrectly) from 1997 to 2000, and the Enron stock price went up during this time period, income was incorrectly recorded by Enron since JEDI owned Enron stock. The adjustment to the earnings of 1997–2000 were to a large extent the result of not consolidating Chewco and JEDI, thus allowing the gains in Enron stock owned by JEDI to affect Enron's incomes. The consolidation was not required because it was assumed that Barclay had made the necessary equity investment leading to an independent Chewco and an independent JEDI.

Adding to the complexity is the fact that Barclay's equity investments were called "certificates" and "funding agreements". They paid "yield" and not interest. While this was not an unusual practice for SPE financing (see p. 50), a reasonable interpretation would be that Barclay's investment was not exactly equity. If the SPE did not take a tax deduction for the "yield" paid this would be an indicator that the SPE considered the security to be equity.

The reductions in income caused by the newly revealed necessity to consolidate Chewco and JEDI were as follows (p. 42):

Year	Reported Net Income	Reduction in Net Income
1997	$105	$28
1998	703	133
1999	839	153
2000	979	91
Total	$2626	$405

It is interesting to note that this entire confusion was caused by Chewco for not being able to raise $6.6 million of independent equity. It would appear that Ken Lay was not asked to raise this capital since one would assume that this would be an easy task for him in 1997.

JEDI's Management Fee

JEDI paid Enron an annual management fee, and income was recorded by Enron as the services were rendered (p. 57). Enron and Chewco later amended the partnership agreement "to convert 80% of the annual fee to a required payment to Enron". In 1998, Enron recorded a $28 million asset (the net present value of the required payment through June 2003) and recognized $25.7 million as income. Only the 1998 portion should have been recognized as income; thus the income for 1998 was overstated by approximately $20 million (pre-tax) for this transaction. Income should not have been recognized before the service was rendered.

The Gains of Kopper

Kopper received $2 million for fees and for managing Chewco from December 1997 through December 2000. Chewco paid $300,000 per year to SONR #1 L.P., and Kopper was the only manager of SONR #1. SONR #1 received a total of $1.6 million from Chewco for management fees. When Enron repurchased Chewco's interest in JEDI in March 2001 Kopper and Dodson made more than $10 million from the Enron purchase.

The disadvantage of not having an arms length transaction is that it becomes impossible to distinguish legitimate payments from shady deals. There were too many potential conflicts of interest.

Kopper and Dodson made a $125,000 investment in Chewco. They received approximately $7.5 million cash during the life of the investment plus $3 million cash at termination; "this represents an internal rate of return of more than 360%". It does not include the $1.6 million of management fees received by Kopper, and the buyout was tax-free to Chewco (p. 64). There was a $2.6 million payment made by Enron to Chewco to pay the income taxes of Kopper and Dodson. Enron counsel advised Fastow that this payment was not required under the Agreement but it was made.

Since Kopper was an Enron employee, the $125,000 equity investment was not independent equity; thus Chewco also had to be consolidated only considering this factor.

Accusations of Evil-Doing

The creation of Chewco is an important example of an action that Enron's top management must regret. Chewco was created because of a perceived necessity not to consolidate JEDI. Without consolidation, the debt of JEDI did not appear on Enron's balance sheet, but JEDI's income was reported there. This income was generated to a large extent from the Enron common stock owned by JEDI during the period when Enron stock increased in value. With consolidation, there would be no income from Enron stock appreciation. In fact, even without consolidation many accountants would argue strongly against Enron including as income the price appreciation on Enron stock owned by JEDI, an Enron subsidiary. In fact, in the third quarter of 2000 Arthur Andersen decided that it was improper to continue to record this type of economic change as income.

Secondly, Chewco was organized by two Enron employees, Fastow and Kopper. This arrangement was not approved by Enron's Board. The conflict of interest situation should not have been allowed (we know this with hindsight, but the likelihood of problems should have been anticipated). Also, it can be argued that Enron (or its employees) controlled Chewco; thus, it should have been consolidated from 1997 based on the control criterion.

Enron guaranteed Chewco debt. A debt guarantee deserves a prominent display.

Consolidation should have taken place in 1997–2001 given that the Barclay investment was not all equity because of the cash "reserve" it demanded. Also, the Kopper equity investment was not independent. It would seem that prior to 2001 Arthur Andersen did not recognize the necessity to consolidate. Was Enron aware that failure to consolidate was an error? Who, in Enron, realized that faulty accounting was taking place? Was anyone at Arthur Andersen aware before 2001 of the fact that $6.6 million of Barclay's equity investment was effectively not equity?

Errors were made that could have been avoided if Enron had not bought out CALPERS' investment (thus Chewco would not have been created).

Secondly, even if CALPERS were bought out, if JEDI had been consolidated, the gains on Enron stock would not have been shown as income.

Third, if Chewco or its equivalent was to be created, it should have been created by independent parties, not Enron employees.

The creation of Chewco, and the way it was used was wrong, but hardly the sort of actions that should lead to the severity of criticisms from the news media and by the Congressional hearings.

The existence of Chewco was revealed to the public by *The Wall Street Journal* (26 October 2001). Chewco came into existence in 1997. But it is possible that it was in October 2001 that Arthur Andersen first became aware that Chewco did not have the outside (independent) equity that allowed it not to be consolidated. When did Enron's accounting people become aware that Chewco and JEDI should have been consolidated? This is relevant in determining the amount of wrongdoing. Further, did the Board of Directors know that Michael Kopper, an employee of Enron, was involved with Chewco? There is conjecture that the Board did not know that Mr Kopper was involved with Chewco and thus the Board did not waive the conflict of interest policy with regard to Kopper.

Robert K. Jaedicke (Chairman of the Board's Audit Committee), in his testimony before the Subcommittee on Oversight and Investigations of the Committee on Energy and Commerce (US House of Representatives, 7 February 2002, p. 7) stated:

> I do not recall the Board ever being made aware that Chewco was an affiliated transaction until last fall, and the Special Committee apparently found no evidence of anyone informing the Board of this critical fact.
>
> The board had relied on senior management and its external advisors, including Arthur Andersen and Vinson & Elkins, to structure and account for the Chewco transaction. The Board had no reason to question the accounting for the Chewco transaction because, as far as the Board knew, Chewco was entirely unaffiliated with Enron, and Enron's internal and external auditors would ensure that it was properly accounted for.

Jaedicke goes on to state:

> Yet these internal and external controls failed to bring to the Board's attention the critical fact that Michael Kopper, an Enron employee, had an interest in Chewco. To the contrary, the representation made to the Board was that Chewco was a completely unaffiliated third party.

Herbert S. Winokur, Jr's testimony to the same committee on the same date included the following:

> There is no suggestion in the Report that any Board member knew that Chewco was, in fact, an affiliated transaction.
>
> Plainly, however, this fact was known to Vinson & Elkins. They drafted the transaction documents that created Michael Kopper's interest in this transaction. That interest, it is undisputed, was a violation of Enron's Code of Conduct. It was never presented to or authorized by the Board.
>
> Andrew Fastow and Michael Kopper both knew this violated the Code. It appears that this was known to other Enron employees within the legal department as well (p. 15).

The report that is referred to is the Powers Report.

The Importance of Chewco

Chewco is important because of its impact on Enron's income. If Chewco had been consolidated, this income overstatement would not have happened.

Did Fastow and Kopper understand that Chewco should have been consolidated? Did they have criminal intent? Remember that the revelation of Chewco income overstatement was a prime factor leading to Enron's bankruptcy.

To what extent was the law firm Vineon & Elkins responsible given that they prepared transaction documents that created Kopper's interest in Chewco? Would Fastow have involved V&E if he knew what was being done was illegal?

Conclusions

Richard III lost his kingdom for the lack of a nail. Ken Lay was tripped up by Chewco and JEDI. They lacked $6.6 million of independent equity (or $6.7 million if the Kopper investment is not accepted as independent equity).

Let us consider the nature of the offenses with Chewco.

(a) Related parties.   This structure should have been avoided but in itself is not corruption. However, failure to obtain Board approval for Chewco and for the participation of Kopper was a major error.

(b) Failure to consolidate the three subsidiaries.   An observer had to know that 3% independent equity was required for Enron not to consolidate. In addition, the observer had to know that $6.6 million of Barclay's $11.4 million equity investment was disqualified, as was Kopper's $125,000; thus consolidation was required since 1997.

(c) The involvement of Fastow and Kopper meant there was not independence for Chewco and it should have been consolidated since 1997.

(d) The gain on Enron stock owned by JEDI reported as income. It can be argued that the gains on the Enron stock is not income for Enron. Arthur Andersen, in 2000, concluded that there should not be an income effect for Enron from Enron's stock price increase on the stock owned by JEDI. The gains on Enron stock should have been excluded from Enron's income from 1997, to 2001.

If JEDI and Chewco should be consolidated (as was concluded in October 2001) then Enron should not have included the gains on Enron stock held as an investment by an Enron consolidated subsidiary. Since JEDI should have been consolidated since 1997, the $405 million of adjustments to Enron's income for 1997–2001 for the Chewco transactions were appropriate. If Barclay's investment had been all independent equity and the Kopper investment did not exist, and Kopper was not involved with Chewco, Chewco would not have to be consolidated and Enron might argue that the reporting of the Enron investment stock gains as income by Enron was acceptable (but not optimum). Historically, a corporation has not been allowed to report as income gains from holding its own stock. Even if the gains on the stock were earned by a nonconsolidated subsidiary of Enron (JEDI) it is not good accounting for Enron to report those gains as income. Andersen finally agreed with this conclusion in the third quarter of 2000.

On 19 April 2002, David Duncan (partner in charge of the Enron account for Arthur Andersen) pleaded guilty to one felony charge of obstruction of justice. This criminal act was the destruction of documents related to Arthur Andersen's work for Enron.

Duncan still took the position that he (thus Arthur Andersen) was not aware of the transactions that involved Chewco.

Chapter 8

LJM1 and Rhythms*

LJM1 was formed with Enron's Board approval in June 1999 with Andrew Fastow as the general partner. LJM1 had three purposes:

1. To hedge Enron's investment in Rhythms (Rhythms Net Communications, Inc.).
2. To purchase part of Enron's Brazilian power project.
3. To buy part of a SPE called "Osprey Trust."

Restricted Enron stock was "sold" by Enron to LJM1 in exchange for a note receivable. LJM2 was formed by Fastow in October 1999.

We will focus on the attempt by Enron to hedge its Rhythms equity investment.

The Board Approval

In June 1999, the Enron Board voted to allow Andrew S Fastow to create several nonconsolidated partnerships. It was claimed that the move would allow debt to be removed from Enron's balance sheet, create an opportunity to sell Enron assets more rapidly, and the partnerships would be useful hedging vehicles.

---

*All the page references in this chapter are to the Powers Report unless otherwise indicated.

In May 2000, the Board was told by Fastow that the partnerships had contributed over $200 million to Enron's earnings.

While an internal document indicates that Arthur Andersen had concerns relative to Enron's accounting for the partnerships as early as February 2001, Arthur Andersen did not share those concerns with the Board at that time. Since the Arthur Andersen document has not been published, we do not know whether or not Andersen was at fault for not informing the board. Perhaps it was already too late for Enron by February 2001.

A board member Robert Jaedicke (Testimony of 7 February 2002), defended the approval of LJM transactions (pp. 7–8):

> "As noted in the Report, LJM1 and LJM2 were presented to the Board as having significant benefits to Enron. The Office of the Chairman determined that the LJM structure — with Mr. Fastow as the general partner of the LJMs — would not adversely affect the interests of the company. Senior management discussed with the Board the very real and substantial benefits to Enron of such a structure. The Board thought, based upon these presentations, that the LJM partnerships offered real business benefits to Enron that outweighed the potential risks. Even today, the Special Committee recognizes — as did the Board when it approved the LJM structure — that significant and legitimate economic benefits were presented to justify why Mr Fastow should be permitted to assume the role that we ultimately permitted him to assume. The Special Committee can disagree with the Board's weighing of the benefits and potential risks of the LJM structure, but it cannot fairly be characterized as a decision that the Board was not entitled to make".

Jaedicke points out that the Board approved Fastow's participation in LJM but "did not waive Enron's Code of Business Conduct".

While the Board was "entitled" to make the decision that created LJM1 and LJM2, with the assistance of hindsight, we know that the Enron Corporation would have been better off without the two partnerships.

Rhythms and Enron

In March 1998, Enron purchased 5.4 million shares of Rhythms at $1.85 per share. On 7 April 1999, Rhythms went public at a price of $21. By the end of the day the Rhythms stock reached $69 per share. The total market value of the Rhythms stock was $373 million.

Enron was prohibited by the agreement with the Rhythms Corporation from selling the Rhythms stock prior to the end of 1999. The Rhythms stock was marked to market by Enron thus the stock price increase gave rise to a large amount of income (approximately $369 million) for Enron and increased the risks associated with the investment and could result in fluctuations in accounting income of Enron.

Enron wanted to hedge the Rhythms stock given the large stock price increase and the risks associated with the investment and future stock price changes. It tried to buy puts but it could not find counterparties at reasonable prices for these put transactions. The market for Rhythms stock was too thin and just as Enron could not use the capital market to hedge, other parties also would find it impossible (or very difficult and expensive) to hedge their positions. The primary reason for creating LJM1 was to set up a SPE called LJM Swap Sub, LP, whose function was to sell put options to Enron on the 5.4 million shares of Rhythms stock owned by Enron. When Enron owned the put options on 5.4 million shares, Enron was hedged. Or was it?

A Valid Hypothetical Hedge

Let us consider a hypothetical situation where Swap Sub was independent of Enron and it sold to Enron 5.4 million puts for Rhythms stock with an exercise price of $56. To insure the ability to pay the put liability with 100% probability Swap Sub would need $302 million of liquid assets.

$$\$56(5.4) = \$302 \text{ million}.$$

With $302 million of liquid assets, if the price of Rhythms stock were to go to zero, Swap Sub could pay $302 million to Enron. The Rhythms stock (5.4 million shares) would be hedged for any stock price drop below the exercise price of $56.

The Enron "Hedge"

Now, we will return from the hypothetical hedge situation to where LJM Swap Sub, L.P., has Fastow as a general partner and whose sole director is Andrew Fastow.

Fastow arranges for Enron to transfer forward contracts for Enron stock to LJM Cayman L.P. (LJM1) in exchange for a $64 million note payables by LJM1. LJM1 also raises $16 million of cash from groups of investors.

Enron placed restrictions on the Enron shares held by LJM1 (they could not be sold or transferred for four years and the Enron stock could not be hedged for one year). Without restrictions, the shares had a value of $276 million. The value of the shares was discounted by 39% (approximately $108 million) in the transaction because of the above restrictions. The net value of the forward contracts with restrictions was approximately $168 million. LJM1 gave Enron a note for $64 million. You are probably wondering why LJM1 could pay only $64 million for stock worth either $276 million (unrestricted) or $168 million (restricted). LJM1 also arranged for Enron to receive a put option on 5.4 million shares of Rhythms stock from Swap Sub.

The value of the put option was estimated to be $104 million. Add the $64 million note and we have LJM1 paying $168 million for the restricted stock worth $168 million. Given the difficulties of valuing the put option, the restricted stock, and the note receivable, the magnitudes of the amounts paid and received seem to be reasonable. Price Waterhouse Coopers supplied Enron with a fairness opinion of the transaction.

Later the terms were adjusted by increasing the note payable to Enron and adjusting the terms of the put option (see p. 82).

LJM1 invests $3.75 million cash and forward contracts for 1.6 million shares of Enron stock in Swap Sub. Swap Sub sells the equivalent of put options on 5.4 million shares of Rhythms stock to Enron. The exercise price was $56 per share and the puts matured in June 2004.

The only assets of Swap Sub were the forward contracts for 1.6 million shares of Enron stock and $3.75 million cash. The forward contracts for 1.6 million shares of Enron stock had a market value of approximately $80 million in 1999.

To be 100% sure of paying Enron and honoring the put options on 5.4 million shares, Swap Sub would need liquid assets of $302.4 million

$$5.4(\$56) = \$302,400,000.$$

This calculation of $302,400,000 of possible liability assumes a zero stock price for Rhythms. Swap Sub has $83.75 million of assets, including $80 million of forward contracts on Enron stock, but this $83.75 million is not an accurate measure of Swap Sub's ability to pay if the put is exercised.

Rhythms stock is a major asset of Enron. If Rhythms stock goes down in value, the value of the puts owned by Enron goes up. But, the ability of the Swap Sub to pay off the puts goes down since without valid puts on Rhythms stock, the value of Enron stock goes down when the value of Rhythms goes down. The prime asset of Swap Sub is Enron stock.

The hedge established by setting up Swap Sub and selling puts to Enron was not worthy of the name "hedge". It was not an effective economic hedge since the assets owned by Swap Sub were highly correlated with the value of the asset being hedged.

Swap Sub could pay off the put if Rhythms stock went down a dollar or two but if the price decrease was large the ability of Swap Sub to pay was significantly compromised.

A Price Decline

Now assume Rhythms stock falls in value by a significant amount. Assume Enron's top management have been told that hedges exist. A loss is recognized on Rhythms stock as the stock is marked to market.

However, a gain is recorded on the put, given that a hedge exists. The net result is zero for Enron given the existence of a hedge.

But assume that the information is revealed that LJM Swap Sub does not have the assets to pay off the put. The gain on the puts is not a real gain since Swap Sub does not own real independent assets. It owns Enron stock that falls in value as the Rhythms stock falls in value. Now the loss on Rhythms stock is not balanced by a gain on the puts that were supposed to offset losses on the Rhythms stock price decline.

Forward Contacts

Enron purchased forward contracts from major banks to buy Enron stock at a fixed price. Since the Enron stock price went up, the forward contracts increased in value. Enron gave forward contracts for 3.4 million shares of Enron stock to LJM1 (a value of $276 million). In exchange LJM1 gave a note to Enron. LJM1 transferred 1.6 million of the Enron shares to Swap Sub for $3.75 million cash. Also, Enron received from Swap Sub a put option on 5.4 million shares of Rhythms stock.

Buying of Forward Contracts

Enron bought forward contracts on Enron stock. The stated purpose was to hedge the dilution resulting from its employee stock options program. Any stock option program dilutes the initial outstanding shares. Buying forward contracts is a gamble on future stock prices, but does not reduce the dilution.

Assume a stock is sold at $20 per share and that the members of the management are given options to buy at $25 one year hence. The company buys a forward to buy a share at $25 one year later.

If the stock price is $40 at time one, the company executes the forward contract and has a $15 gain on the forward (the $40 stock is bought at $25). However, the firm sells a share worth $40 to management at a price of $25 thus has a $15 loss on the giving of the option.

Now assume the stock price is $10 at time one. The company loses $15 on the forward contract (it buys a stock worth $10 for $25). Management does not exercise the option to buy at $25.

Buying the forward contract results in the firm losing if the price at time one is less than $25. If the price at time one is greater than $25, the firm wins on the forward and loses on having given management options.

Consolidation

Swap Sub had $83.75 million of assets ($80 million of restricted Enron stock and $3.75 million of cash) and $104 million of potential put option liability on Rhythms stock. Lacking 3% of independent equity, it probably should have been consolidated in 1999. In October 2001, Arthur Andersen decided that Swap Sub should have been consolidated in 1999. The failure to consolidate could have been based on valuing the Enron stock owned by Swap Sub on an unrestricted basis.

Unwinding: Rhythms

In the first quarter of 2000, Enron moved to liquidate its Rhythms position (p. 87). This could mean the sale of Rhythms stock or it could mean the elimination of the puts on Rhythms stock issued by Swap Sub. Enron was no longer blocked from selling the Rhythms stock.

On 8 March 2000, Enron gave Swap Sub a put on 3.1 million shares of Enron stock with an exercise price of $71.31. The current stock price was $71.31 at the time of agreement and was $67.19 when the contract was signed. Swap Sub (p. 88) "did not pay any option premium or provide any other consideration in exchange for the put." Given that the put was in the money by $4.12 million on the day the contract was executed and Enron was giving Swap Sub a put for 3.1 million shares, explanations are needed as to why Enron made the gift of the puts.

The unwind agreement was dated 22 March 2000. The major terms of the agreement were:

1. Termination of the put option on Rhythms stock held by Enron (having an estimated value of $207 million).
2. Swap Sub returned 3.1 million Enron shares to Enron (having an unrestricted value of $234 million).
3. Enron paid $16.7 million to Swap Sub.

The $16.7 million payment was computed as follows:

The agreed amount		$30.00
Dividend on Enron stock		0.50
		$30.50
Less cash held by Swap Sub	$3.75	
Loan and interest	10.10	$13.85
Net		$16.65

The logic of the $30 million "agreed amount" is not clear. It is the basis of a "huge windfall" (p. 89) to Swap Sub and LJM1. Both Skilling and Lay claim to be unaware of the terms of the unwind agreement. No fairness opinion was obtained for the unwind. The Board does not seem to have been informed.

The Rhythms put options at the time of the unwind had a value of $207 million. Swap Sub returned Enron shares having an "unrestricted value" of $234 million. Swap Sub also received $27 million cash. These Enron shares were not unrestricted. The original discount (in June 1999) amortized would be approximately $72 million. Swap Sub benefited by approximately $72 million.

After the unwind, LJM1 still retained 3.6 million Enron shares with a value of $251 million (unrestricted).

Conflicts with Banks

Assume that you are the Managing Director of an investment bank seeking to do business with Enron and earn hefty fees. The CFO of

Enron asks whether you (or your bank) would be willing to invest in LJM. The Enron CFO is investing in and organizing LJM.

You would certainly weigh the other benefits from investing in LJM besides the direct expected internal rate of return. The related party organization of LJM meant that conflicts of interest were inevitable. For every bank that rejected the LJM deal because of conflict of interests, there would be other banks or bank officers saying "yes they would invest."

The Controls

Jaedicke (2002, pp. 8–9) lists the controls that the Board established for LJM. They include the following (taken from his testimony):

1. "Enron and LJM had no obligation to do business with each other.
2. Enron's Chief Accounting Officer, Mr. Fastow's equal in the corporate structure, was to review and approve any transactions.
3. Enron's Chief Risk Officer, also Mr. Fastow's equal in the corporate structure, was to review and approve any transactions.
4. Jeff Skilling, President and Chief Operating Officer, and Mr Fastow's superior also was to review and approve any transactions.
5. Arthur Andersen was involved from the beginning in structuring and accounting for these transactions to ensure that they were done properly.
6. Once a year the Audit Committee reviewed the transactions that had been completed in the prior year.
7. An LJM Approval Process Checklist was to be filled out to ensure compliance with the Board's directive for transacting with LJM, including questions regarding alternative sales options, a determination that the transaction was conducted at arms-length, and review of the transaction by Enron's Office of the Chairman, Chief Accounting Officer and Chief Risk Officer.

8. Enron employees who reported to Mr Fastow were not permitted to negotiate with LJM on behalf of Enron.
9. The Commercial, Legal and Accounting departments of Enron Global Finance were to monitor compliance with the procedures and controls, and were to regularly update the Chief Accounting and Risk Officers.
10. Mr Fastow was not relieved of his fiduciary duties to Enron.
11. The Office of the Chairman of the Board could ask Mr Fastow to resign from LJM at any time.
12. Mr Skilling was to review Mr. Fastow's economic interest in Enron and LJM.
13. Enron's internal and outside counsel were to regularly consult regarding disclosure obligations concerning LJM, and were to review any such disclosures".

Jaedicke also listed seven major facts that were concealed from the Board (page 10 of his testimony).

Winokur's testimony (7 February 2002) was consistent with that of Jaedicke (p. 3):

"A number of senior Enron employees, we now know, did not tell us the full truth. Our accountants at Arthur Andersen, and our lawyers at Vinson & Elkins, we now know, did not provide good advice to us. The related party arrangements were terribly abused. I feel, however, that the tragedy of Enron's bankruptcy might well have been avoided if the controls we put in place had been followed as we intended, and if the important transactions about which we were not informed had not occurred. But I assure you that my colleagues and I, at the time, did our best to understand the risks and benefits involved in permitting Mr Fastow to become the general partner of the LJM partnerships".

Winokur discussed the unwinding of the Rhythms transaction (p. 15):

> "The decision to unwind the Rhythms transaction was not disclosed to the Board. Our requirement that all related party transactions be reported to the Audit Committee therefore was violated.
>
> This, too, is a transaction that was grossly unfair on its face — but, as the Special Committee report states, we simply didn't know about it. I am horrified that Mr Fastow and other employees of Enron apparently have profited, secretly, at Enron's expense as a result of this transaction. I am particularly unhappy that Enron employees were permitted to participate in what clearly seems to be a corporate opportunity".

Winokur was also a member of Enron's board of directors.

An Illustrative Example

Assume Parent has an investment in stock of start-up worth $300 million, the value of which it would like to hedge. It creates a SPE called Swap Sub. Swap Sub has one asset $200 million of Parent common stock and $200 million of stock equity. Swap Sub has sold puts to Parent with an exercise price of $300 million (the put proceeds were used to buy Parent stock).

First, assume the value of start-up stock decreases to $280 million. The puts have a value of $20 million at maturity. Swap Sub sells $20 million of Parent stock and pays Parent $20 million. Parent has a loss of $20 on its investment in start-up stock and a gain of $20 on the puts (the cost of the puts is an expense).

Now assume the start-up stock goes down in value to $15 million. This is a loss for Parent of $285 million. The puts it holds would have a value of $285 million except the only asset of Swap Sub is Parent stock initially worth $200 million. Assume this stock has fallen in value to $50 million. Swap Sub can pay $50 million to Parent. The hedge fell apart because the loss was too large and because Swap Sub's only asset, Parent stock, decreased in value. The hedge was not effective with a large decrease in start-up's value or a large decrease in Parent's stock value.

The Enron situation with LJM1 and Rhythms was analogous to this simplified example. Did the top management of Enron really think they had an effective hedge?

We have a multiple choice question. Enron top management was

a. In the dark regarding LJM1 (with the exception of Fastow).
b. Understood the transactions but thought there was a valid hedge.
c. Understood the transactions but thought they could fool others into thinking there was a hedge.

Did you choose a, b, or c? The US Government chose c (implying that Lay and Skilling understood there was not an effective economic hedge).

Conclusions

As long as Rhythms stock did not fall in value by a significant amount, the arrangement with Swap Sub gave the appearance of being an effective hedge. When Rhythms stock fell significantly, the partial hedge fell apart. Given that the primary asset of Swap Sub was Enron stock the structure of the hedge was flawed. The bad accounting (recognizing Enron's gain on the put) was linked to the bad financial structure of the partial economic hedge.

In November 2001, Enron and Arthur Andersen concluded that the SPE involved in selling puts to Enron failed the test for nonconsolidation. The accounting in 1999, 2000, and the first half of 2001 was incorrect. This revision reduced Enron's net income for 1999 by $95 million (of $893 million) and for 2000 by $8 million (of $979 million) (p. 16).

The Rhythms "hedge" was terminated in 2000. The Powers Report states (p. 16) "These investors walked away with tens of millions of dollars in value that, in an arm's-length context, Enron would never have given away". Fastow took care of his interests, Kopper and four other Enron employees.

How the investors made money by investing in LJM1 and selling puts in stocks that decreased in value would be a mystery if we did not have the Enron Chief Financial Officer Fastow deciding on the terms of termination under which the Swap Sub (and the prime investor, Fastow), would be allowed out of the put contracts that had lost hundreds of millions.

Once Fastow was allowed to invest in entities doing business with Enron it was likely that there would be conflicts of interest, or the appearance of conflicts. The termination of the Rhythms contract is a very severe illustration of self-interest affecting the negotiation. Andrew Fastow received more than $30 million of cash flow from LJM1 and LJM2 (p. 3).

"Kopper and his coinvestors in Chewco received more than $10 million from Enron for a $125,000 investment" (p. 26). Imagine what they would have earned if Chewco had been profitable.

George F Will wrote (*Newsweek*, 28 January 2002, p. 64) "Enron's prosperity was a bubble produced by trickery and pricked by reality". A nice dramatic sentence, but not completely accurate. The majority of the prosperity was real, not a bubble. Unfortunately, a large part of prosperity was linked to common stock prices, that can go down as well as up. The trickery came when Enron tried to protect the gains it had properly recorded. It was the failure to record promptly (in a timely fashion) the subsequent losses that gave rise to the need for adjustments to past period's earnings.

The Editorial of the 18 January 2002 issue of *The Wall Street Journal* illustrates the confusion regarding the purpose of the partnerships:

> "The details of Enron's now famous off-balance-sheet partnerships remain murky. But it's clear they were an attempt to disguise losses from bad investments".

In actual fact, the purpose was to preserve frequently the gains on good investments that could not be sold. The investments had appreciated but now losses would be reported as the values went down. If the hedges had been effective, they would have made it unnecessary to report losses if the value of the Rhythms stock had gone down since there would have been balancing gains in the hedges. Unfortunately, the hedges were not effective since the value of the assets of the entity selling the puts would decrease as the value of the asset (Rhythms stock) decreased.

Chapter 9

LJM2 and Raptors I and III*

In October 1999, LJM2 was formed by Andrew Fastow. The Raptors were financed and managed by LJM2. There were finally four SPEs called Raptor. Enron's Board of Directors waived its rules to allow Andrew Fastow to serve as LJM2's general partner. Investors were told that they could expect to earn annual returns of 30% or more. JEDI had returned 20% in excess per year for CALPERS. Earnings were to be distributed as they were earned with the result that the equity investor's risk was reduced with these distributions. LJM2 had approximately 50 limited partners. The partners invested $394 million. The LJM partnerships entered into more than 20 transactions with Enron. If Fastow controlled either LJM1 or LJM2, the controlled unit(s) should have been consolidated from the date of initiation. Fastow was the CFO of Enron. LJM2 provided the "independent" equity to avoid consolidation of the Raptors, but since there was no independence they should have been consolidated.

The Raptors sold Enron puts on many of its merchant investments. Enron "sold" its stock (or stock contracts) to three of the Raptors at a discount (it was restricted stock). Also, Raptor III received from Enron shares of the TNPC stock held as an investment by Enron. The transactions with the Raptors affected Enron's reported incomes of the two years, 2000 and 2001. One estimate is that $1.1 billion should

---

*All the page references in this chapter are to the Powers Report unless otherwise indicated.

be deducted from Enron's reported 2000–2001 income to adjust for Raptor transactions. This deduction would reduce the 2000–2001 incomes to $429 million (before tax).

Merrill Lynch, in 1999, was chosen to raise capital for LJM2 and it raised $394 million. Investors expected to earn 30% a year or more. Some of the returns exceeded 100%. The general partners did even better. Kopper was also given a $3.8 million management fee (which was contested). Kopper's participation had not been approved by the Board.

Winokur was a member of Enron's board of directors. His testimony (7 February 2002) regarding Raptors included the following ("Report" refers to the Powers Report):

> "The Report makes clear that this transaction was materially and deliberately misrepresented to the Board. Throughout the Board minutes and in the presentation materials, the Board was assured that the projected return for this transaction was 30%. In fact, as is evident from Deal Approval sheets signed by Ben Glisan, and Scott Sefton, management of the company knew that LJM's projected return was, in fact, a minimum of 76%. Mr Fastow also must have known these facts, because they were presented to the partners of LJM2 at their annual meeting. Both Mr Gilsan and Mr Fastow attended the Board meeting where Raptor was presented. Neither of them told us the true rate of return they had projected".

Significant returns were earned by LJM2 by buying assets from Enron and selling them back at higher prices. Fastow, of course, was involved with setting both prices. The fact that Fastow would be involved was used by Merrill to sell the partnership to outside investors (the list of outside investors includes many, but not all, of Wall Street's finest).

Even though the Raptor deals ultimately lost money (by selling puts on assets that decreased in value), by then LJM2 had already returned cash to its investors so that the investors made extremely large returns. One of the most valuable assets owned by the partnership was a natural gas pipeline between Canada and the United States.

It would be interesting to know exactly how Merrill was able to attract $394 million from very sophisticated investors for a partnership that was going to own a few real assets with very volatile value and was going to sell puts on other (or the same) volatile assets. Obviously, Merrill promised the expectation of high returns, but how were these returns to be earned?

The New York Times (4 January 2002, p. 13) presented an excerpt from a document used by Merrill to attract investors to consider LJM2:

> "Due to their active involvement in the investment activities of Enron, the Principals will be in an advantageous position to analyze potential investments for LJM2. The Principals, as senior financial officers of Enron, will typically be familiar with the investment opportunities the Partnership considers. The Principals believe that their access to Enron's information pertaining to potential investments will contribute to superior returns".

LJM2 is destined to be the highpoint of the Enron collapse for those seeking villains. It would appear that a material amount of Enron's value was drained off by the LJM2 partnership. The outside investors merely cashed their checks. The inside investors made sure that the cash flowed.

Let us consider the magnitude of the cash drain from Enron. Starting with the initial $394 million equity investment and assume a 40% return payable in each of the 2 years.

$$0.40(394) = \$158 \text{ million}$$
$$\times 2$$
$$\$316 \text{ million}$$

A 20% return for the 2 years would be one half of $316 million or $158 million.

The New York Times (31 March 2002, p. 20) estimated that the limited partners earned an annual return of 43%. This 43% return was earned during a time period when corporate bonds yielded less than 10%.

LJM2 was a significant factor in Enron's collapse.

The Raptors

An internal document circulated at Enron in the first quarter of 2001 stated "The new Raptor structure transferred risk in the form of stock dilution". Sherron Watkins in a note to Lay added (handwritten) "There it is! That is the smoking gun. You cannot do this!" (*The New York Times*, 15 February 2002, p. C6).

There is no reason to conclude Lay should have understood Watkins' note or the basic document.

The thought that the Raptor "structure transferred risk in the form of stock dilution" is not exactly correct but it is not completely wrong. The Raptors held Enron stock. If this stock was issued to the market, there would be stock dilution. The Raptors sold puts to Enron, this could be a transfer of risk. The puts were on Enron's merchant assets.

A problem arises if the value of the asset for which the put was written falls greatly and the value of the Enron stock also falls. The value of the Raptor's assets decrease at the same time its put liability increases. Then, the Raptor will not be able to pay the put liability. When Miss Watkins writes "You cannot do this!" she is correct if she means that Enron is not protected if there are large losses in the value of its "protected" assets.

Thus, both the basic message being circulated and Miss Watkins' note that was added need extensive explanations. It would be surprising if Ken Lay understood either the basic message or Miss Watkins' note. They are not clearly written.

Raptor I and Enron Puts

Raptor I was created on 18 April 2000. It was given the formal title of Talon LLC (Talon). Raptor I purchased Enron stock and Enron stock contracts (forward contracts) from Enron, which if unrestricted, would have a fair market value of $537 million. The stock was restricted and Talon could not sell, pledge, or hedge the Enron shares for 3 years, thus the stock was valued at $349 million, a 35% discount from the market value.

To simplify the presentation, only the salient facts will be summarized (see Chap. 8 for a more complete description of the transactions of Raptor I).

In exchange for its $537 million (unrestricted stock) or $349 million (restricted stock) Enron received a $400 million note. LJM2 was the manager of Talon and in theory supplied a 3% independent equity that enabled Enron not to consolidate Talon.

Talon had $30 million of cash and $349 to $537 million of Enron stock (the value depends on the amount deducted for restrictions).

If LJM2 did not earn a 30% (annual return) on its $30 million equity investment for the first 6 months, Enron was required to purchase LJM2's interest in Talon based on the unrestricted value of Enron's stock and stock contracts. This modified put held by Talon's equity investment effectively disqualified (from an economic viewpoint) the LJM2 investment from being classified as equity.

To enable Talon to earn the necessary cash flow to pay LJM2, Enron purchased from Talon a put option on Enron stock for $41 million. The put was for 7.2 million shares at a stock price of $57.50 and it expired in 18 October 2000. The Enron stock price when Enron purchased the put was $68 per share.

Why did Enron buy a put on its own stock? (Because it thought the stock price would go down?) Remember, after the $41 million was given to LJM2 by Talon the only assets of Talon were $30 million of cash and $349 to $537 million of Enron stock. For the purpose of illustration, assume Talon held as an asset of 7.9 million shares of Enron stock and $30 million cash. At what price level can Talon still pay its put liability for 7.2 million shares if the exercise price is $57?

Let P be Enron's future stock price. If we include the $400 million note owed by Talon to Enron and assume the 7.9 million restricted shares have a value of P, we have:

$$7.2(57 - P) = 30 + 7.9P - 400$$
$$840.4 = 15.1P$$
$$P = \$55.66.$$

If the Enron price drops to $55.66, Talon cannot pay completely the notes payable and the put. The value of the put to Enron is greatly reduced by the fact that Talon will not be able to pay if there is a large drop in Enron's stock price. If the value of the restricted stock is lesser than P, then the level of Enron stock price, when the put liability can be paid, is even larger.

On 3 August 2000 Talon and Enron settled the put option early with Talon returning $4 million of the $41 million put premium to Enron. Fortunately, the Enron stock had increased in value and the put was out of the money (thus it could be purchased cheaply).

This is a transaction that served little valid economic purpose. Enron bought puts from an entity that had a trivial amount of cash and a large amount of restricted Enron stock. If the value of its put liability went up, the value of its assets (and its ability to pay the put liability) went down. Fastow won if the Enron stock price went up and Enron lost if the Enron stock price went down. There are very few (any?) financial economists who would approve this series of transactions for Enron. Leaving out ethical and legal considerations, they would all approve for Talon's investors the investment of $30 million in Talon and the nearly immediate withdrawal of $41 million earned by selling a put with very limited value. Assume that the $41 million was distributed to equity investors at the end of one year. The investors then earned a 37% annual return on their $30 million equity investment. Only after this return was earned could Talon sell derivatives on Enron's merchant assets (the actual return was much larger than 37% since the time of the distribution of the $41 million was less than a year).

Raptor I and the Hedging of Merchant Investments

The stated objective of the Raptor I hedging activities was not to hedge the economic risk of Enron but to reduce volatility of income (p. 106).

The valid function of accounting practice should be to record economic events and transactions as accurately as possible. When the accounting conflicts with reasonable economic interpretations of events the accounting is faulty.

Enron engaged in "total return swaps" with Talon. Talon would receive any future gains on specified merchant investments and would pay Enron the amount of any future losses. This is normally an acceptable financial arrangement. However, the assumption that Talon would be able to pay if there were merchant investment losses was not valid. Remember, essentially the only assets of Talon were Enron stock. If the value of Enron stock falls greatly Talon cannot pay its obligation on the swap.

The AVICI Swap

The date of the swap for AVICI Systems stock is important. For that, 3 August 2000 was chosen. On that date, the AVICI stock price reached $162.50, its all-time high. If 30 September 2000 had been chosen as a reporting date, Enron would have reported a loss of $67.50 per share if the price of $162.50 had previously been recorded. With 10,000,000 shares of AVICI stock Enron would have reported a loss of $67,500,000. Of course, Talon's profitability was also affected by the date choice.

A decline in Enron stock price accompanied by the decline in AVICI stock value would force Enron to recognize its loss since Talon would not be able to pay its put liability. To prevent Talon from losing if Enron stock fell below $81, Enron entered a contract to pay Talon. If the Enron stock went above $116 per share Talon would pay the gain to Enron. This is alleged to be a "costless collar".

Let us consider the consequence of the Enron stock price falling at the same time of AVICI stock falling. Enron would have a loss if Talon did not protect it. But Talon's asset is Enron stock (or the equivalent) and its value went down. Enron has a contract to pay Talon so that Talon can pay Enron, so Enron pays itself. There is no protection for Enron because of its contract with Talon. The protection is a fiction and loss on AVICI stock should be recognized when it occurs. AVICI lost 98% of its value (from $178 million to $5 million) by the end of 2001.

One must suspect that not only did the complexity of the Talon transactions fool the public it also fooled most, or all, of the Enron managers and the Arthur Andersen auditors.

The New Power Company (TNPC)

TNPC was a power delivery company created by Enron. Enron owned 75% of TNPC.

Enron sold a portion of its equity investment in TNPC to an SPE and recorded a large gain for the sale. It then entered into a total return swap. Enron received any gain or loss and paid a fixed contractual amount. This effectively meant that Enron had not really sold the equity and should not have recorded the gain since there was not a sale of the economic interest.

Enron wanted to hedge its TNPC risk. It chose the total return swap with a counterparty (Raptor III) who could not pay if the TNPC stock fell significantly.

Raptor III

Raptor III was formed to hedge an Enron investment in the common stock of TNPC.

The only assets held by Raptor III was the stock of TNPC (more exactly, Raptor III held warrants to purchase 24 million shares of TNPC stock at a nominal price). Raptor gave Enron a $259 million promissory note in return for TNPC stock. LJM2 invested $30 million and within one week received $39.5 million. Raptor III sold puts to Enron on TNPC stock. Since no Enron stock was involved, Raptor III was not presented to the Enron Board. But it should have been presented.

Did Enron have a hedge?

This is one of the clearest example of a faulty economic hedge used by Enron. It is more outrageous than the Rhythms hedge since it used TNPC stock received from Enron to hedge TNPC stock and the total return swap owned by Enron.

Assume a hypothetical situation where Enron has invested $10,000,000 in TNPC stock and then the stock value went up to $60,000,000. Enron reports a $50,000,000 gain and now wants to hedge.

Enron sells $20,000,000 of TNPC stock (one-third of its holdings) to Raptor III and in return gets puts on its TNPC stock to sell at $40,000,000.

When the TNPC stock falls in value, Enron marks the stock investment to market and has a loss. Fortunately, it balances the loss with a gain on the puts. Unfortunately, the puts are not part of a real economic hedge. This is easiest to see if the TNPC stock goes to zero value. There is a $40,000,000 loss on the stock investment. The put should be worth $40,000,000 but the value of Raptor III's assets is zero. Thus, there is a $40,000,000 loss on the stock investment but no balancing gain on the puts. Returning from the hypothetical, TNPC has lost 80% of its value by the end of 2001.

With this example, how low can TNPC stock fall and still have Raptor III pay its put liability? Assume the value of TNPC stock falls to V where V is less than $40,000,000 (the exercise price of the put). Raptor III now owes $40,000,000 - V$ on the put with a $40,000,000 exercise price and Raptor III's assets are now worth $0.5V$ since Raptor owns 0.5 of the stock that Enron owns. Let us solve for V:

$$40,000,000 - V = 0.5V$$
$$V = 26,667,000.$$

If $V = \$26,667,000$ the maximum value of Enron's puts is $40,000,000 - 26,667,000 = \$13,333,000$. The value of Raptor III's assets if $V = \$26,667,000$ is $0.5(26,667,000) = \$13,333,000$. If V is less than $26,667,000 Raptor III cannot pay its put liability.

There is a partial hedge. Raptor III can pay as long as the value of Enron's TNPC stock does not fall below $26,667,000.

Enron booked the expected proceeds on the TNPC puts; this overstated the incomes of the years 2000 and 2001 since Raptor III did not have the assets to pay the put liability.

Winokur's testimony (7 February 2000) included the following observations regarding Raptor III (p. 12):

> "The Report notes that a vehicle called Raptor III was created by Enron management, purportedly to hedge an investment in New Power stock. The Report makes clear that this transaction was never disclosed to the Board by anyone in management, although it was reviewed by Andersen.
>
> I cannot and will not defend this transaction. It seems obvious to me that one cannot hedge an investment in New Power with warrants on the same New Power stock. It is equally obvious to me that the terms of this transaction, which seem to me to fail to properly value the New Power stock being contributed, were grossly unfair to Enron. We did not know that at the time, and neither company management nor Arthur Andersen — which was involved in valuing this transaction — told us the truth about it".

The IPO

Enron sold the warrants on TNPC stock to Raptor III for $10.75 per share. One week later the initial public offering (IPO) was at a price of $21 per share. At the end of the day the stock price was $27 per share. The SPE paid LJM2 $39.5 million (which then enabled Raptor III to sell put derivatives to Enron).

Enron entered into a total return swap with Raptor III (by way of the SPE owned by Raptor III and LJM2). Raptor III would receive the gains and pay any losses on TNPC stock. Thus Enron no longer worried about the total return swap with the buyer of its equity interests. However, this conclusion requires that the Raptor III counterparty be credit worthy which it cannot be since its only asset is TNPC stock.

The Adjusted Incomes

The Raptors and their hedges were not effective economically and as shown in the following table it affected the incomes of the years 2000 and 2001 materially.

Quarter	Reported earnings (values in millions)	Earnings without raptors' (values in millions)	Raptors' contribution to earnings (values in millions)
3Q 2000	$364	$295	$69
4Q 2000	$286	($176)	$462
1Q 2001	$536	$281	$255
2Q 2001	$530	$490	$40
3Q 2001*	($210)	($461)	$251
	$1506	$429	$1077

*Third quarter 2001 figures exclude the $710 million pretax charge to earnings related to the termination of the Raptors.

Accounting Implications

Consider Raptor III where the SPE held TNPC stock as an asset and the SPE had sold puts on the TNPC stock to Enron. As the TNPC stock price went down, the liability for the put went up and the SPE's ability to pay the liability went down. Obviously, there was no effective economic hedge.

Some (not this author) would argue that there was an accounting hedge. As the TNPC stock price fell, Enron would show a gain on the put that more or less matched the loss on its common stock investment. The fact that the put liability could not be paid by the SPE was not considered. This is faulty accounting even if the written standards were to allow it. The accounting for a hedge should be consistent with the economic characteristics.

The assets of the other three Raptors were Enron stock. Thus, the relationship between the puts and the assets held is not as direct as with Raptor III, but the same general principle applies.

For the last two quarters of 2000, Enron's reported income (pretax) was $650 million. Enron recognized a $500 gain from the puts bought from Raptors. The Raptors could not meet this obligation, thus the gain is overstated.

The Enron stock was transferred to the three Raptors at a discount to the market price since it was restricted stock. The Raptors sold to Enron puts on Enron's merchant investments. It was hoped that the value of the Enron stock would be sufficient to pay the value of the put if the merchant investments decreased in value.

By the first quarter of 2001, the Raptors lacked $500 million in assets to pay the puts (p. 98). "Enron management restructured the vehicles in the first quarter of 2001" (p. 98).

In the spring of 2001, the Raptors were in financial difficulty since the value of Enron's merchant assets had fallen in value dramatically. Fastow arranged a restructuring of the Raptors that avoided the immediate recognition by Enron of some $500 million in losses (Enron held puts that Enron thought would protect it against losses, but the values of the assets of the Raptors were melting rapidly). The restructuring enabled Enron to postpone incorrectly the recognition of losses on its merchant assets until October 2001. The restructuring (see pp. 122–125) had the Raptors helping to finance each other and, in addition, Enron offered additional Enron stock and contracts. There were no real assets injected to solve the problem of the merchant assets decreasing in value.

In the third quarter of 2001, Enron closed down the Raptors and recognize belatedly a $544 million after tax charge (part of the 16 October 2001 disclosures).

The Powers Report (p. 99) says that from the third quarter of 2000 through the third quarter of 2001 "Transactions with the Raptors during that period allowed Enron to avoid reflecting on its income statement almost $1 billion in losses on its merchant investments". The Enron earnings for the last two quarters of 2000 and first three quarters of 2001 would be reduced to $429 million (pretax), a decline of 72% (p. 99).

Raptor Restructuring

As long as the assets of the Raptors (stock of Enron and TNPC) were larger than the net gain that Enron earned on the puts it had purchased, Enron could offset the losses it was suffering on merchant investments.

To keep any one Raptor from being unable to meet its derivative obligations, Enron used the credit capacity of the other Raptors. It is far from clear that this entire process was justification for not recording market losses on the merchant investments that already occurred.

There is an 12 October 2001 memorandum from the Arthur Andersen partners (Chicago office) advising that the process being used "was not a permissible means to avoid a credit reserve loss" (p. 120).

The credit problems of 2000 and the first quarter of 2001 are described as the "Raptors' credit capacity problem" (p. 121). This is not accurate. The problem was that the merchant investments had lost value and the Raptors had sold puts to Enron on these assets. Enron worked at fixing the Raptor credit problem and the problem was not real. It was all aimed at hiding the merchant investment losses which following mark-to-market accounting should have been recognized.

In March 2001, Enron was faced with the fact that the Raptors did not have sufficient assets to cover their put liabilities. To avoid having to recognize $500 million of merchant asset losses Enron transferred $828 million of forward contracts to the Raptors. Thus, Enron was in effect paying itself so that it could avoid reporting the merchant asset losses.

The "Costless Collar"

To define a costless collar, assume an investor owns a stock. The investor can sell a call option on all gains above the defined exercise price. The investor receives cash for selling the call.

The investor wants to protect against a stock price fall, thus the investor buys a put option (an option to sell the stock at the put exercise price).

The exercise price of the call and the exercise price of the put are set so that the cash proceeds from the call exactly equal to the cost of the put. Thus, we have a costless collar (for the given exercise prices). By selling the upside, the downside (below the exercise price) is eliminated.

In October 2000, Enron entered into a costless collar with Talon. Talon bought puts on the 7.6 million Enron stock (and stock contracts) it owned with an exercise price of $81 per share. If the Enron stock price fell because the value of the merchant assets fell, Talon was now protected and could pay the put liability. Enron would pay Talon but Talon owned a put option on Enron stock.

In summary, Enron would pay Talon which would pay Enron. The puts held by Enron and Talon effectively cancelled each other.

The End of the Raptors

In September 2001, Kenneth Lay decided to terminate the Raptors. Enron paid LJM2 approximately $35 million. Valuing the Enron stock, the restricted Enron stock, and the collars on Enron stock was complex and obviously one can object to the magnitude of the payment to LJM2.

In 2000 and 2001, Enron had recognized $1.1 billion of gain from transactions with the Raptors. There was a charge of $710 million as a result of the unwinding. This still left $390 million of pretax earnings.

The New Power Holdings

On 11 June 2002, The New Power Holdings Inc., filed for bankruptcy protection (Chap. 11). At the time, it had 520,000 customers.

Conclusions

LJM2 was formed in October 1999. The general partners were Andrew Fastow, Michael Kooper, and Benjamin Glisan. Outside investors included insurance companies, banks, and investment banks. Merrill Lynch underwrote the LJM2 equity offering. LJM2 invested in the Raptors. The Raptors bought real assets from Enron (such as power plants and gas pipelines) as well as stock that Enron had purchased (merchant assets) and Enron stock. Enron agreed to supply more Enron stock if the value of the Raptor investments fell or if its liabilities increased.

In September 2000, LJM2 sold "puts" to Enron. The puts enabled Enron to sell its stock to LJM2 at a fixed price anytime in the following six months. But it was not obvious that LJM2 could buy the stock.

If bad things happened and Enron's stock price went down, the value of the puts owned by Enron would go up. It was a hedge except for one complexity. If the major asset of the LJM2 was the investment in the Raptors and if the Raptors were invested in Enron stock (or the equivalent), the Raptors would not be able to pay its liability for the puts. Fortunately, LJM2 and Enron arranged an early settlement of the put contracts before Enron stock fell below the exercise price of the puts. LJM2 actually made a gain from the sales of the puts to Enron.

On some of the other put contracts bought by Enron from the Raptors of LJM2, the Raptors were not so fortunate. The Raptors could not pay the put liabilities as the value of the Raptor assets declined in the fall of 2000. Enron supplied more of its common stock to the Raptors but the value of Enron's common stock was also falling with the result that the Raptors still could not pay. This sequence of events led to the 16 October 2001 third quarter loss.

The adjustments that had to be made to income in October and November 2001 originated in a failure to consolidate two entities (Chewco and JEDI) with the result that their gains from holding Enron stock were reported as income for Enron.

Second, there was a series of SPEs set up to hedge Enron merchant assets. Unfortunately the hedges were effective for a narrow range of stock prices with the result that gains were recorded on puts which were not really gains and should not have been recorded as Enron income. The puts were sold by a party which could not make the payment if the investment being protected well in value by a large amount.

The Raptors were terminated in September 2001. This termination resulted in the 16 October 2001 announcement of a $544 after-tax charge against earnings by Enron. The $544 deduction resulted because of the gains from the puts owned by Enron did not really exist. The Raptors did not have the assets to pay the put liabilities.

The Powers Report estimated the effect of the partial hedges on the income of the Raptors to be almost $1 billion.

> "We believe these transactions resulted in Enron reporting earnings from the third quarter of 2000 through the third quarter of 2001 that were almost $1 billion higher than should have been reported" (p. 4).

The Raptors were complex financial vehicles created with the objective of enabling Enron not to report losses from its merchant investments. When the Raptors were created it was not certain that losses would occur but there was a possibility. Remember, the function of the Raptors was not to prevent the losses from occurring. It was merely to prevent the accounting reports from presenting these losses if they did occur.

The Raptors needed independent investors so that the affairs of the Raptors were not to be consolidated with the affairs of Enron. The investors in the Raptors made very large returns far in excess of the return available in the capital market. These returns were made possible by Andrew Fastow.

Thus, Enron paid a large real price (in cash) to create and operate the Raptors whose primary function was effectively to mislead the readers of Enron's financial statements.

The Powers Report describes in detail the seven specific accounting issues raised by the accounting practices of Enron with respect to the Raptors (pp. 129–132). But there is an even more important issue. All accountants understand that the primary function of accounting is to report the economic consequences of events and transactions. There are rules (called Generally Accepted Accounting Principles) that have evolved through the years to insure that the function is accomplished effectively. The Enron CFO attempted to use these rules, not to communicate useful financial information, but to hide information if it was not favorable.

Go to an oceanside sandy beach and watch a young child build a wall of sand to hold back the ocean. The actions of Enron to prevent reporting a loss on its stock or a loss on the merchant assets it owned were comparable. It constructed the equivalent of a sand wall by buying puts from entities whose value was going to decrease as the asset being protected has lost its value.

Fastow offered explanations for Enron's use of off balance sheet debt (*The New York Times*, 18 January 2002, p. C7)

> "If a company like Enron has too much debt on its balance sheet, then the rating agencies will lower Enron Corp.'s rating". Mr Fastow said. "So, we endeavor to find ways to finance activities off balance sheet".

In addition, there is a transfer of risk.

> "In making things off balance sheet", Mr Fastow said, "you're actually transferring risks of the transaction to investors. So when you sell something to investors, they take some risk, they earn a return from that risk".

These explanations stop short of justifying a situation where Enron subsidiaries were used to attempt to eliminate risk on Enron assets. Labeling this attempt as an "accounting hedge" rather than an "economic hedge" is merely an effort to ignore the fact that there was not an effective hedge. Enron accounting reported income as if Enron had effectively hedged against losses on its merchant assets. But, it had not effectively hedged.

These transactions are clearly bad finance and bad accounting. The US Government also decided that these transactions were also criminal and brought charges against Fastow.

Chapter 10

LJM2 and Raptors II and IV*

Raptors II and IV were authorized on 22 June 2000, and were then given contingent contracts to obtain Enron shares (forward contracts) and in return these two Raptors engaged in derivative transactions with Enron to protect its merchant investments. The primary objective was to provide "P&L protection," i.e., allow the accountants to record transactions as if there were actual economic hedges. LJM2 owned Raptors II and IV.

The Contingent Contracts

Raptor II received the rights to 7.8 million Enron shares and Raptor IV received the rights to 6.3 million shares. If on 1 March 2003 the Enron stock price was above $63 per share Raptor II would receive 7.8 million shares. If it was above $76 per share Raptor IV would receive all 6.3 million shares. A different number of shares would be issued for prices below $63 and $76 (p. 111).

Raptor II could not write derivatives with Enron until LJM2 received its $41 million of cash flow (in excess of a 30% return).

Each of the Raptors-owned SPEs that contracted with Enron but for simplification these entities (Timberwolf and Bobcat) will not be

---

*All the page references in this chapter are to the Powers Report or to the Skilling–Lay trial proceedings.

used here and it will be assumed that the transactions were completed directly with the Raptors. Both Raptor II and Raptor IV received $41 million from Enron for put options on Enron's merchant investments.

The put options were settled early and both Raptors distributed little less than $41 million to LJM2. The puts were out of the money.

The two Raptors entered into costless collars with Enron (see Chap. 9 for an explanation).

Asset Sales to LJM2

From September 1999 through July 2001 (when Fastow sold his interest in LJM2 to Kopper) Enron sold and bought back assets to LJM2. The purposes of these sales might include:

a. Removing debt from Enron's balance sheet.
b. Recording gains on the sales.
c. Rationalizing the Enron business structure.
d. Generating cash.

It is likely that the first two reasons were the prime motivations for most of the transactions. For example, Enron bought back five of the seven assets sold during the last two quarters of 1999 (p. 124). Fastow reported to the Board's Finance Committee that these transactions generated $229 million of earnings in the second half of 1999 (Enron recorded $549 million after tax earnings in that period).

There is an evidence that LJM2 was guaranteed a profit in some of these transactions implying that there were not truly sales in those situations.

Analysis of the sales to LJM2 and the repurchases is tainted by the fact that Fastow, the CFO of Enron, was involved as an investor and manager of the other side of the transactions. What could have been transactions accomplished for good business reasons became suspect given the related party aspects of the transactions.

The churned transactions were noted by Winokur (p. 14).

> "The report notes that there was an observable pattern of assets being sold to LJM in one quarter, with earnings

being booked, only to be repurchased by Enron in the following quarter. This, too, was concealed from the Board".

Winokur's testimony relative to the Raptor recapitalization was (pp. 12–13):

"The credit problems with the Raptor entities which began in late 2000 were not disclosed to the Board. The decision in early 2001 to recapitalize the Raptor structure with an $800 million forward contract on Enron stock was, likewise, concealed from us".

Given its magnitude, and the critical issues it raised, this transaction is one that should have required Board approval. The existing risk-management mechanisms also should have, but did not, reveal this to the Board. At each Finance Committee meeting, Mr Rich Buy, senior vice president at Enron, and head of the Risk Assessment and Control Department, presented to the Finance Committee a list of the Top 25 credit exposures for Enron. In February 2001, when the Raptors were allegedly $350 million underwater, neither Raptor nor LJM appeared on the list that Mr Buy presented to the Finance Committee, nor did he, Mr Fastow, or Mr Skilling, all of whom were in attendance at that meeting, raise this matter.

As has been disclosed in the press early in January 2001, Arthur Andersen held an internal meeting in which it expressed significant concern about the credit capacity of the Raptor vehicles and the quality of the earnings being attributed to them. Just 1 week later, however, with full knowledge of the Raptor credit problems, Arthur Andersen assured the Audit Committee that Enron would receive a clean audit opinion on its financials.

The Board and LJM1 and LJM2

Jaedicke's testimony (7 February 2002) lists seven facts about LJM1 and LJM2 that appear to have been concealed from the Board (pp. 10–11):

1. "As with Chewco, the Board did not know that Michael Kopper was involved in LJM. According to the report, the Private Placement Memorandum — which was reviewed by Enron's in-house lawyers and by Vinson & Elkins — indicates that Michael Kopper would be involved in managing LJM's day-to-day activities. Both Enron's in-house lawyers and Vinson & Elkins, Enron's outside counsel, apparently reviewed this memorandum, but failed to inform the Board of what they learned.

2. The Board was not informed of and did not approve any other Enron employees — besides Mr Fastow — working for or having a financial interest in LJM. It turns out that number of other employees — in violation of the Enron Code of Conduct — did work for or took a financial interest in LJM.

3. The Board was not told that Enron sold seven assets to LJM1 and LJM2 in the third and fourth quarter of 1999, and then turned around and repurchased five of those seven assets after the financial reporting period closed. I do not believe any of those repurchase transactions were presented to the Board for review.

4. The Board was not told that Enron agreed to protect LJM from losses on any of its transactions with LJM.

5. The Board was not told that the requirement that only employees who did not report to Fastow could negotiate with LJM on behalf of Enron was ignored.

6. In early 2001, the Board was not told that the Raptor transactions were several hundred million dollars undercapitalized, or that management therefore intended to restructure those transactions requiring issuance of some 800 million additional shares of Enron stock.

7. Finally, the senior management and external advisors of Enron, on whom the Board relied for information,

never reported to the Board that any of the LJM transactions were unfair to Enron, involved questionable
terms, or violated any accounting rules. Instead, the
Board and the Audit Committee were regularly told by
those who had no personal stake in LJM that all of the
controls were functioning properly, and that all of the
transactions being done were properly accounted for,
were at arms length and were fair to Enron".

Naming the SPE

You might well wonder the origin of the name LJM. Andrew Fastow's
wife was Lea and his two sons were Jeffrey and Mathew, thus LJM.
Adding to the suspicion that Fastow was not aware that he was committing crimes is the fact that one of his prime vehicles for criminal
acts was named for his family.

The Termination

The Raptors were terminated in September 2001. Revelations regarding the Raptors resulted in the 16 October 2001 announcement of
the $544 million after-tax charge against Enron's earnings. The effort
made by Enron to hedge its merchant assets with the homemade
ad hoc Raptors was a failure when the value changes were larger than
the changes anticipated by Enron management.

The Trial

The LJM deals and the accounting for LJM events were the number 1
factor leading to Enron's bankruptcy. Ms Ruemmler attempted to
connect Skilling and Lay directly to the LJM transactions (p. 17782):

"You've seen — you've seen evidence in the case that the
LJM transactions between Enron and LJM were supposed
to be approved by the office of the chairman, either Mr
Skilling or Mr Lay".

But there was no proof Skilling and Lay initiated LJM transactions (Fastow did) and Ms Ruemmler observed (p. 17783):

> "Despite all of that evidence that Mr. Skilling and/or Mr. Lay were supposed to approve these deals, you know that the vast majority of the approval sheets were never signed. I think one or two were signed, but the vast majority were not".

The existence of the LJM units was not a crime. We can disagree strongly with several hedging strategies (they were bad finance) but it is not clear that they were established with criminal intent. The accounting errors (failure to consolidate) could very well have been unintentional, and not criminal.

Aside from Fastow and his friends receiving unsightly gains from the LJM transactions, it is difficult to tie Skilling and Lay to criminal acts regarding the LJM units.

Conclusions

Raptors II and IV were structured in a manner similar to Raptor I. The objective of the Raptors was to eliminate the volatility in accounting income using a hedge device that was not an effective hedge. It was a situation where bad accounting was used to report a bad economic transaction. The hedge would melt away in a situation where the Enron stock price fell significantly. The SPE would receive cash and Enron stock from Enron for the puts. The SPE would then be able to pay Enron if the value of the puts increased by small amounts. There was effectively no protection for the merchant investments being protected by Raptors II and IV for large value changes.

The Raptors were complex financial vehicles created with the objective of enabling Enron not to report losses from its merchant investments. When the Raptors were created it was not certain that losses would occur but there was a possibility. Remember, the function of the Raptors was not to prevent the losses from occurring. It was merely to prevent the accounting reports from presenting these losses if they did occur.

The Raptors needed independent investors so that the affairs of the Raptors were not to be consolidated with the affairs of Enron. The investors in the Raptors made very large returns far in excess of the return available in the capital market. These returns were made possible by Andrew Fastow.

Thus, Enron paid a large real price (in cash) to create and operate the Raptors whose primary function was to mislead the readers of Enron's financial statements.

The Powers Report discusses in detail the seven specific accounting issues raised by the accounting practices of Enron with respect to the Raptors (pp. 129–132). But there is an even more important issue. All accountants understand that the primary function of accounting is to report the economic consequences of events and transactions. There are rules (called Generally Accepted Accounting Principles) that have evolved through the years to insure that the accounting function is accomplished more effectively. The Enron CFO attempted to use these rules, not to communicate useful financial information, but to hide information if it was not favorable.

Winokur's testimony (7 February 2002) states (p. 17):

> "All transactions with LJM were required to be on terms that were fair to Enron and negotiated at arm's length. Had that requirement been adhered to, none of the unfair transactions criticized in the report could — or should — have occurred".

But with the assistance of hindsight, Winokur should realize that allowing a conflict of interest situation to be created led to a series of events that could easily have been avoided by not having created a conflict of interest situation.

Chapter 11

Other Transactions

There are a large number of miscellaneous accounting and finance transactions of Enron that at a minimum raise questions about Enron's desire to communicate accurate and understandable financial information.

Prepaid Swaps

The New York Times (17 February 2002, p. 1) described several transactions that one finds difficult to accept as they are described.

Consider a prepaid swap. Citigroup gave Enron $2.4 million and Enron was obligated to repay the cash over five years. If it walks like a duck, it is a duck. This swap is a loan and Enron should have shown it as a debt. If it did not, its accounting was in error. I do not know how Enron accounted for the swap, but I know how they should have. The obligation to repay over five years the initial amount received was a debt. The name of the transaction is not relevant.

Based on published financial documents we cannot determine if Enron's accounting for this type of debt was faulty. Failure to record a liability for the swap transaction described would be an error.

Swaps of Capacity

It is possible for two corporations to swap capacity and use the swap to inflate revenues and income.

Assume Firm A has excess Fiber Optic Capacity in one location and sells it at an artificially high price to Firm B. Firm A records a large gain. But Firm B sells excess capacity at an artificially high price to Firm A, and B records a large gain.

Both firms record large revenues and large gains, but no net cash changes hands. If the sale prices are not based on economic facts (market prices) there is intent to mislead and both firms are guilty of operating in a dishonest manner.

The difficulty is in determining whether both firms colluded in setting artificial prices, and inflating incomes.

Did Enron ever do transactions analogous to those described above?

Enron Energy Services

The Energy Services division sold electricity and natural gas to commercial and industrial customers. One of its senior officers was Thomas E. White, who became the Secretary of the Army in June 2001. As a member of the Bush administration he had to sell his Enron stock at the high prices as of August 2001.

It was alleged that the Energy Services Division would book profits if it had a contract and expected the price of electricity to fall in the future (*The New York Times*, 25 January 2002). This is such bad accounting I prefer to hope that the *Times* misunderstood the explanation offered by an Enron employee. If gains were recorded because it was estimated that prices might fall in the future, that would clearly be an accounting error. Income should not be recorded because it is hoped that the costs will drop in the future.

Accounting theory requires that profits be recorded as the services are rendered. Expenses are also recorded as the services are rendered and revenues are earned. Recording profits when the contract was signed when future expenses are not known would not be acceptable accounting.

If incomes were recorded for long-term energy contracts at the time of signing the contract, it is very probable that some incomes were recorded for contracts that were not going to be profitable. Labeling the recognition of unrealized income as mark-to-market accounting is to misuse the term.

The Trial

Ms Ruemmler stresses the importance of EES in establishing the alleged criminal activities of Skilling and Lay (p. 17716):

> So let's start with EES. What's the bottom line with EES? You heard a lot of evidence about Enron Energy Services. That was Enron's retail business. It was one of the principal growth engines for the stock price. Mr Skilling, Mr Lay were very committed to it. It, along with broadband, were going to be the principal drivers of the increase in stock price.

Ms Ruemmler stresses that the EES story had to be told optimistically to maintain the Enron stock price. Consider the following quote where Lay's comments to Enron employees are strongly described by Ms Ruemmler as "the outside story". (p. 17716):

> The outside message: EES was an incredible success. Over 2000 and 2001, it was increasing profitability quarter-on-quarter. As Mr Lay told the employees in August of 2001, "EES just keeps banging away. Just keeps growing at a tremendous rate. Most importantly, net profits are growing." This was the outside story. Critically important to the Enron stock price. You heard that from witness after witness after witness.
>
> What was the reality? The reality: EES was a basket case. Mr Delainey told you, when he took over as CEO, he quickly learned that it was — it needed to be retooled in flight. It had suffered hundreds of millions of dollars in losses.

Are there really investors who make investment decisions based on the optimistic forecasts of the firm's Chairman and CEO? That is truly a crime.

Consider the following statements by Ms Ruemmler (pp. 17718–17719):

> Mr Skilling at an analysts conference tells the investors that he projects that, by the end of 2001, retail will be worth $23 a share. ... It's not criminal, ladies and gentlemen, to make a prediction that turns out not to be true. And the Judge instructed you to that effect.
>
> What's important about this — what's important about this $23 a share is that Mr Skilling and Mr Lay needed EES to succeed. They were telling the market 'Value our stock at $126 a share. That's what we think it will be worth. And $23 of it is EES.'
>
> EES's success was incredibly important to the Enron story and to the Enron stock price. That $23 a share is the motive for why EES failed. Mr Skilling and Mr Lay had to cover up the failure.

The US Attorneys had to prove that there was criminal intent in the comments made by Skilling and Lay regarding EES. It is difficult to believe that any investor used Skilling's $23 a share value estimate for EES as the basis of a buy decision for Enron stock, but the US Government thought that it loomed large.

A second issue was the source of EES' income (p. 17720):

> Ms Rieker, you will recall, testified that she told Mr Lay that in the fall of 2000. She said to Mr Lay, "Look, I'm concerned about the message that we're giving to the investors about EES because they're not really making money from their actual business operations. They're making it from these structured finance transactions."

While it is desirable that corporations reveal how they make their earnings, I would not send a manager to prison because he/she did not make clear the source of each dollar of income.

Consider the issue of whether losses on wholesale trade should be charged to EES or to wholesale (p. 17722):

> There was a decision made to move those trades and that associated book that they called the wholesale supply book over to wholesale. That was — that decision was made early, early in the quarter. The key thing for you to remember, ladies and gentlemen, is that that decision to move those trades and that book from EES to wholesale is a totally different decision that — the one that was made in Mr Skilling's office on March 29th that you've heard a lot about.

Do we know that moving the trades from EES to wholesale is a criminal act?

The White Affair

The Secretary of the Army, T. E. White may be one of the luckiest people in the world. He sold 380,000 Enron shares for more than $10,000,000 by 30 October 2001 either to satisfy the ethics considerations of his position or to exploit the high stock price. In one more month's time the stock would have been worth close to zero. In August 2001, Mr White asked the Senate to give him time until 1 January 2002 to complete the sale of his investments or to exercise his options. The Senate Armed Services Committee refused his request and required White to sell the shares he owned immediately.

If he had a desire to delay the sale of his stock, we would say that Mr White was not aware of Enron's financial difficulties in August 2001. If the delay was to give his stock options time to increase in value, the request for the delay was more self-serving but misguided.

The Southampton Place Partnership

This partnership was formed by Andrew S. Fastow and Michael J. Kopper. Other Enron employees also invested in Southampton.

The investors made large returns on their investments. The gains were the result of negotiations between Enron employees some of whom were also Southampton investors. This was a bad arrangement with inherent conflicts of interest.

The Bonuses

Many Enron executives were paid generous bonuses in 2001 based on Enron stock price and earning targets. But these earnings were later adjusted downward (as were the earnings of 1997–2000). What action should be taken regarding the bonuses that were paid, but based on revised earnings, were not earned? For example, Andrew Fastow was paid $3,036,000 in bonuses in the first 2 months of 2001.

Other Transactions

In this book, I have reviewed selected events and transactions. There are many omissions since they tend to repeat the basic nature of the transactions described. For example, LJM had transactions with Cuiaba (Brazil), ENA CLO, Nowa Sarzyn (Poland), MEGS (Gulf of Mexico), Yosemite (a trust), backbone (Broadband), and many others (see pp. 146–147 of Powers Report for 13 other transactions). These transactions were not central to Enron's bankruptcy or to the Skilling–Lay trial.

There were many transactions where it is likely that revenues were accelerated and expenses deferred and debts were hidden. The rules of accounting were stretched beyond reason or logic, by Enron.

Conclusions

Accounting is partly science and partly art, but there are some transactions where there is agreement among professionals as to the correct accounting treatment. We do not know for sure that Enron violated well-known and respected accounting rules (in addition to those already acknowledged) but there is reason to suspect that the accounting for recording (or not recording) debt and the timing of revenue and expense recognition was not as good as we would like them to be.

Chapter 12

The Collapse

There are many facets to the Enron case. Some contributed directly and some indirectly to Enron's collapse. Some are interesting, but did not lead to the collapse. On 10 January 2002, Arthur Andersen admitted that it shredded Enron documents in October 2001. On 15 January 2002, the NYSE removed Enron from its trading and listing.

Factors That Did Not Cause the Collapse

The related party transactions were inappropriate and it is likely that the rewards to the related parties were excessive, but the approximately $50,000,000 taken by the Enron employees from the SPEs, that did business with Enron, did not directly cause Enron's bankruptcy (it did contribute to the loss of faith in Enron management). The use of SPEs in general does not imply anything good or bad about a corporation. Knowing Enron used a large number of SPEs tells us very little. How the SPEs were used is important.

Lay sold shares of Enron stock throughout 2001. This could be an example of selling based on inside information, but it is more likely to be the result of a sensible effort to diversify or to obtain cash to pay loans that were due as a result of falling stock prices.

First, the mark-to-market accounting led to the reporting of large gains on merchant investments and other financial transactions.

Then, it led to efforts to maintain those gains. Not all the efforts to hedge the gains were appropriate. But the mark-to-market accounting should not be blamed because of subsequent inappropriate actions by Enron management, and that it was sometimes applied inappropriately where there were no explicit market prices.

Financial analysts were still recommending Enron stock as a "buy" as late as October 2001. Given that most of the information regarding the overstatement of earnings was not revealed until 16 October 2001, recommendations given before that date can be forgiven. Recommendations after that date were not to be praised but certainly can be forgiven if based on a perceived underlying soundness of Enron's operations.

With the aid of hindsight, we know that the Board of Directors should have controlled Fastow more effectively. In fact, they should not have allowed the related parties to do business with Enron. Given the persuasive arguments offered by Fastow to establish the LJM1 and LJM2 entities it is understandable why permission was given. It is unlikely that the nature of these entities and their functions were understood by Lay. Maybe Skilling understood.

Factors Contributing Indirectly

It is interesting that the initially successful merchant investments of Enron contributed indirectly to Enron's collapse. Both the Rhythms NetConnections Company and The New Power Company stocks increased greatly in value after Enron made investments in them. These increases in value were reported as income by Enron following the mark-to-market accounting. It was Enron's efforts to hedge these unrealized gains (for accounting purposes) that led Enron to stretch the accounting rules.

Factors Leading to Collapse

The factors leading to Enron's collapse included:

1. Bad real investments created uncertainty about Enron's financial health. The shaky investments included the Dabhol Power

Company in India, the Cuiaba power plant in Brazil, and the investment in water companies by Azurix.
2. The broadband trading and retail energy (EES) had not yet become profitable.
3. When real hedge could not be obtained for Rhythms, accounting hedges were constructed that lacked theoretical validity (they were not effective economic hedges).
4. When a real hedge could not be obtained for TNPC, accounting hedges were constructed that were almost laughable in their ineffectiveness as hedges (the hedging entities had TNPC stock as their primary asset).
5. A significant percentage of Enron's income for 1999 and 2000 reflected increases in the value of Enron stock held by an Enron-controlled subsidiary. This resulted from the misguided efforts to hedge the gains on the Rhythms investment and faulty accounting.
6. Failure to consolidate three entities that should have been consolidated led to the adjustment of earnings of 1997 through the first half of 2001 when consolidation was retroactively required.
7. Revelations of related party transactions and the large incomes on those transactions earned by the Enron CFO (Andrew Fastow) and a few other Enron employees.
8. The news media emphasized Enron's misdeeds in excess of their economic significance to Enron.
9. The creditors and trading partners fled from Enron with the result that there were large third and fourth quarter losses in 2001.
10. The financial community concluded that given the bad news reported by Enron in October and November 2001, there was probably more bad news to come. In December 2001, Enron declared bankruptcy.

Jaedicke's testimony (7 February 2002) included the following (p. 2):

As stated in the Report of the Special Committee, internal management and outside advisors did not raise concerns with the Board; regularly assured us that the transactions had been reviewed and that they were lawful and appropriate.

It is now clear that management and the outside consultants failed to disclose critical information about these transactions of which they were clearly aware.

After reading the Report, I would like to add that if even some of the Board's controls had worked as expected, I believe that we could have addressed these issues and avoided this terrible tragedy.

The report that is referred to is the Powers Report.

The Accounting

Enron's accounting reports were frequently opaque. The footnotes to the year 2000 annual report leave too much to the readers' imagination.

Enron pushed the limits of accounting. Thus, the use of accounting hedges that did not come close to being effective economic hedges, but were effectively a way to avoid reporting the mark-to-market losses on merchant assets as long as the losses were not large. Enron also exploited and exceeded the rules of consolidation (maybe accidentally) to avoid consolidating its SPEs. Changes in the rules were needed.

Does a firm have a responsibility to have its accounting meet a higher standard than the generally accepted accounting principles? There are many problems with firms defining standards rather than having its accounting consistent with the accepted standard. For example, comparability between firms could be lost. Also, the firm-specific improved accounting may not actually be an improvement.

Mark-to-Market Accounting

Assume a corporation has a marketable common stock that it paid $60 to acquire. At the end of the year the market price is $90. The mark-to-market accounting would record $30 of income.

Now assume a firm has a contract to supply natural gas for the next 20 years at a given price. The cost of the gas will fluctuate through time. Unless there are comparable contracts being traded there is no well-defined market price and the mark-to-market rule cannot be reliably applied. Enron tried to apply it.

The FASB has defended its due process approach, taking the time to consider the views of all interested parties. It will now have to consider ways to accelerate its decision process without giving up the benefits of considering a variety of viewpoints. The rules for consolidation and the rules for mark-to-market accounting need adjustment.

A Summary of Accounting Issues

The Enron collapse calls our attention to several different accounting issues that are worthy of review. These include:

1. The accounting for SPEs. The 3% of equity and the independence requirement need modification and stiffening.
2. Guarantees of debt need to be better understood and possibly be included on the firm's balance sheet.
3. The rules of consolidation need review (especially where there are elements of control).
4. The gains on a firm's own stock should not flow back to its income statement even if a nonconsolidated but related entity owns the stock.
5. A sale of an asset is not a sale if the buyer has the right to put (sell) the asset back at a defined price.
6. The mark-to-market accounting should not be used if there are no clearly defined market prices.
7. The auditor should insist on understandable information footnotes.
8. The sources of the incomes should be disclosed if the sources are unusual (not the result of normal operations).
9. Conflicts of interest situations should be fully disclosed.

The 401K Mess

Enron employees could invest up to 6% of their base pay in the investments of their choice. If they chose Enron stock they bought it at market price, however, the company increased the investment and reduced the cost per share by contributing an amount of Enron stock equity to 50% of the investment of the employee. This arrangement or a variation of it was standard for a large number of corporations. Unfortunately it discourages investment diversification by employees. Also, there were defined periods where the employees could not sell their Enron stock. Enron (as many companies) encouraged the investment in its own stock.

While a quick reading might lead one to conclude that the employees are buying Enron stock at half price, they are actually buying at 67% of the market price. Let C be the cost per share of a stock sold at $60, then:

$$(1 + 0.5)C = 60,$$

$$C = \$40 \text{ per share.}$$

The cost per share to the employee is 67% of the market price.

On 17 October 2002, the company changed the 401(k) pension plan administrator. The change prevented all pension plan participants from selling their Enron stock for 30 days. The decision to change the administrator might have been made earlier, but the timing was disastrous for those employees wanting to sell their Enron stock in October and November 2001.

Enron Really Lost Money

Enron had a major financial exposure in Brazil. Since 1998, it invested approximately $3 billion in an electric distribution company and other projects. It will be lucky if it (or its successor) will get a $0.50 on $1 of investment. Enron and its partners invested $2.9 billion in the Dabhol plant in India, and Enron owned 0.65 of the project. GE and Bechtel each owned 0.10, and Maharashtra State Electricity Board owned 0.15. The investment was a disaster. The Indian electricity customer refused to pay the price for electricity that Enron required. The plant was shut down.

In 1998, Enron bought Wessex Water for $1.9 billion. It hoped to establish a market to buy and sell water. On March 2002 Enron sold Wessex Water to a Malaysian company for $777 million. If a firm loses a billion here and a billion there, pretty soon it becomes material. It is not clear how buying a water company in England enables a corporation to trade water contracts on a worldwide basis.

There were also investments in Mexico and Poland that did not lead to required returns. Enron's entry into the trading of Broadband capacity was losing a lot of money (there was excess capacity while Enron forecasted a shortage of capacity). In July 2000, Enron and Blockbuster formed a partnership to provide movies (video) on demand to customers anywhere in the world via the internet. The stock market liked the idea (the Enron stock price reached $90). In March 2001, Enron and Blockbuster threw in the towel and gave up on their vision to supply movies on demand.

In summary, Enron lost money in the old-fashioned way, investing in real assets and paying too much for those assets. It was not clever financing that caused these losses, but rather bad bets on developing economies and the relentless nature of competition.

Feeble Humor

Searching for humor (no matter how slight)? Consider that Jeffrey K Skilling's lawyer was Bruce Hiler, and Sherron Watkin's lawyer was Philip Hilder. Thus, we have (*The New York Times*, 2 March 2002) "Philip Hilder, called Mr Hiler's contentions 'pathetic'". A proofreader will have problems given the closeness of the names.

A Neglected Signal

In 1999, I was given a prospectus of a bond issue. The bonds issued were to finance the acquisition of a water company by a major corporation. The bonds were unique since they raised capital and gave rise to a tax deduction, but no debt was added to the parent's balance sheet. I turned these facts into a case for my advanced corporate finance course.

The course evaluations recommended dropping the case since the conclusions were not worth the time spent. The case was "Marlin" (see the figure that follows):

The Marlin Transactions

The following chart illustrates the structure of the Marlin Transactions. The chart does not purport to be complete and is qualified in its entirety by, and should be read in conjunction with, the more detailed information regarding the Marlin Transactions included elsewhere in this Offering Memorandum and the Transaction Documents described herein. Amounts are in millions of US dollars.

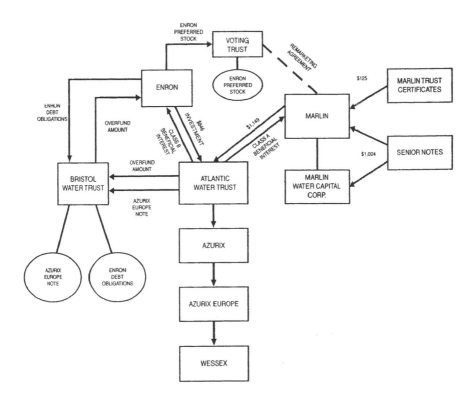

I made a mistake. The details of Marlin were not worthy of our class time, but the trail led back to Enron, and that would have been worth our attention. I did not see the implications of the Marlin case. The excessive detail of Marlin was worthy of study in order to evaluate Enron, but I did not see it.

Evaluating Arthur Andersen

Let us consider the performance of the accounting firm Arthur Andersen. It destroyed documents related to the Enron collapse. Early in 2002, it was revealed that documents were destroyed in October 2001 after the world was aware that Enron's accounting was faulty and would be investigated.

The author of this book cannot judge the legality of the document shredding, but he does know that at a minimum it was bad public relations. It would be surprising if there were revelations on the shredded documents that were as bad as interested parties thought they were after the shredding.

Arthur's second error was in not keeping Enron's Board aware of its concerns early in 2001 or before. Duncan and others at Arthur Andersen were aware in February 2001 that Enron had significant risks that were not of public knowledge. Why not inform the Enron Board?

Let us assume that Arthur Andersen did not know in 1997 that Chewco did not have 3% independent equity. Thinking Chewco qualified for nonconsolidation it was reasonable not to consolidate Chewco until 2001 when Arthur Andersen found out that Chewco and JEDI should have been consolidated since 1997. Did Arthur Andersen truly find out in 2001 or did it know previously that there was not a 3% independent equity?

There is also the issue of the $1.2 billion entry (debit) to notes receivable and entry to stock equity (credit). Accounting principles do not allow one to record an increase in stock equity balanced by a promise to pay in the future. Recording the increase in stock equity is not acceptable accounting, but it is not a high crime. Why was Arthur Andersen fooled? It is possible that the complex array of SPEs hid the true nature of the transaction until 17 October 2001. Or it could be that Arthur Andersen allowed an incorrect accounting entry. It is very difficult to see why Arthur Andersen would knowingly allow an incorrect accounting entry. It is more likely that the complex manner of structuring the transaction hid the transaction's basic nature.

At what stage should Arthur Andersen have demanded that the curtain be drawn on the Raptors? Before the assets held by Enron decreased in value there was no important accounting issue concerning the Raptors. At some stage the Raptors could no longer honor their put liabilities to Enron. We do not know when this happened, but it was somewhat before October 2001. The Enron Board should have been informed that the puts held by Enron were not fully effective (the SPEs did not have sufficient assets to honor the puts).

There are many issues regarding the recording of debt, the timing of revenues, the timing of expenses, and the recognition of gains on sales of assets, where it is possible that the assets were not actually sold (the buyer had puts to sell back to Enron). We need more information before determining guilt.

Arthur Andersen was tried in the court of public opinion and found guilty before its legal trial. The fact that the US Government indicted the firm did not help Arthur Andersen's customer relations. It became very difficult for a public corporation to hire Arthur Andersen as its auditor. CFOs did not want to defend the choice of Arthur Andersen as the firm's auditor. The fact that Arthur was later found not to be guilty did not help the already dissolved firm.

There is some significant probability that the accounting errors that were made by Enron were not Arthur Andersen's responsibility and that, aside from shredding, no crimes were committed by Arthur Andersen prior to 2001 (whether the shredding was a crime is for history to decide; Andersen was not convicted of that crime). Arthur Andersen, as of May 2002, seems to have gotten a raw deal from the press and the US Justice Department.

Arthur Andersen had a group of outstanding accounting experts available in its Chicago office to answer questions as to the appropriate accounting for difficult issues. This service was available at no cost to any operating office. However, the operating office having received the expert opinion did not have to follow the advice, though it normally did. It is likely that the Chicago experts offered the Houston office advice that could have avoided the issues that ultimately trapped the firm.

Kenneth L Lay

By one definition Lay is responsible for any mistake that was made by an Enron employee. This follows the US Navy tradition that a ship's captain is responsible for anything that happens on the ship. This rule is great in theory because it causes the captain to take a deep interest in all activities that could lead to trouble. Captains of US Navy ships at sea do not get to sleep through the night very often.

Ultimately, a captain is a single person of limited scope. He or she cannot be everywhere. Informed of all possible dangers the captain will soon be exhausted and will become a walking zombie. There are things that happen for which it would not be sensible to hold the captain responsible.

Similarly, Lay delegated responsibilities to Enron's senior officers. Lay retired as the CEO in February 2001 and Skilling was named as the CEO. On 14 August 2001 Skilling resigned for personal reasons. Lay resumed the job of CEO. But Lay was more interested in big issues and the political scene than the details of accounting and finance as they applied to Enron.

Lay hired Skilling and Fastow to take care of the accounting and finance. The accounting problems that ultimately led to the need to revise the operating results for 1997–2001 (first half) were very technical. Now, the world is aware of the nature of Enron's accounting problems, there will be differences of opinion as to whether or not Enron should have been allowed to record the entries that they did.

Even though, when Enron was in error as with Chewco, it was an error because of a technicality. Chewco failed to have a 3% independent equity, that should have been consolidated. But why 3%? Also, how is the 3% to be measured and what should be included as equity? The rules should have been followed, but these rules were not carried down by Moses from the Mount.

There is no reason today to conclude that Lay was consistently on top of Enron's accounting and financial manipulations. I doubt if it will ever be proven that Lay adequately understood Chewco, JEDI, and the Raptors. But he allowed these units to exist and that was an error.

During 2001, Lay sold shares of Enron stock. We can intuit a combination of three motivations for the sales:

a. Need for cash (to repay loans).
b. Need for diversification.
c. Inside information that Enron was headed for financial problems.

We do not know the weightings for each of the above motivations. We hope that inside information was not a factor, but it is not possible to exclude the possibility that Lay saw that Enron's financial situation that was weak and becoming weaker and he then decided to diversify.

Jeffrey Skilling

We do not know what Skilling knew and when he knew it. We do know that Skilling is both intelligent and knowledgeable regarding business strategies and transactions. It is difficult to believe that he was not aware of Fastow's use of the SPEs. But he did not seem to do anything that led to Enron's bankruptcy. In the trial (2006), it was shown that he was too often too optimistic, but that is expected of a corporate president.

Andrew Fastow

Andrew Fastow is a puzzle. He did so many things as CFO that he should not have done.

Consider LJM1 and LJM2, these two vehicles were studied intensively to determine the crimes that were committed. Both LJMs used initials of Fastow's wife and children. If he intended to do something that was not completely ethical or legal would he tack his family's initials on the vehicle for the wrongdoing?

It is entirely possible that Fastow thought everything he did was legal and ethical but that he merely had bad judgment combined with bad luck. The world is likely to think differently. The legal system convicted him.

If the value of Enron's merchant assets had gone up in 2000 and 2001 and Enron's stock had increased in value (or not gone down), Chewco, JEDI, and the Raptors had prospered Fastow might have pulled the great escape. But even then, much of what Enron did in accounting and finance was not "right" and different actions would have been preferred. He should have kept the Board informed and he should have recognized the sensitive position he was in when he effectively was negotiating with himself.

Keep in mind that there were enough losses on real assets to cause Enron to suffer financial distress. The amount taken by Fastow and friends was relatively small.

On 2 October 2002, Andrew Fastow was charged with fraud (hiding debt, inflating Enron's profits, and of illegal personal monetary gains). Among the vehicles used were LJM, Southampton, and Chewco.

Having implied that Andrew Fastow was the evil key figure in Enron's collapse, let us balance the picture somewhat by revealing that he was the third base coach for his 7-year-old son's baseball team (summer 2002). He was not all bad.

Three Transactions

There were three very questionable deals at Enron that we have not discussed in depths that might well be fraud (likely Fastow and maybe Skilling and Lay).

Enron owned more than 50% of a company building a power plant in Cuiaba, Brazil. LJM bought 13% of the plant for $11.3 million in 1999. In 2001, Enron bought back its investment for $13.7 million (the buyback might have been a part of the deal to sell).

In 1999, Enron sold rights to Nigerian barges to Merrill Lynch for $7 million. In 2000 (6 months later), Enron bought Merrill's ownership for $7.5 million. The price was probably prearranged. LJM2 received a fee.

Enron owned 1.09 million shares of Avici Systems. The price of the stock went up. To protect its gain, Enron bought puts from Raptor 1. Raptor 1 was a subsidiary of Talon which was financed by Enron and LJM2. It is alleged that LJM2 was guaranteed a significant profit.

While all three of these deals were very suspect, we do not know for sure that Skilling and/or Lay knew and understood the details.

The International Bubble

Rebecca Mark's international activities led to Enron being very exposed to financial problems since these investments were made as a part of a grandiose master long-term strategy and premiums were paid for these assets. These assets totaled in excess of $10 billion. Enron was not able to sell these assets rapidly in the fall of 2001. Thus Ms Ruemmler states (p. 17694):

> "Mr Lay and Mr Skilling had been unable to sell $10 billion or so in international assets that were dragging the company down. Mr Skilling had estimated that those assets were worth only about half of what they were being carried on Enron's books for. An expensive venture into Enron's — into the water business — you heard about this — Azurix was just a colossal disaster".

Skilling was not a fan of Ms Mark and would probably understate the value of the assets that she had accumulated. Also, the international assets were acquired at prices in excess of their apparent value, thus from the moment of purchase, they would appear to be overstated on Enron's reports.

The assets of the international group (Rebecca Mark was the CEO of Enron International) were scattered all over the globe. They included (among others):

Dabhol, India (power plant)
Haiman Island, China (power plant)
Marmara, Turkey (power plant)
Bolivia and Brazil (gas pipeline)
Sardina, Italy (power plant)
Poland (power plant)
Philippines (power plant)
Guatemala (power plant)

Guam (power plant)
Colombia (gas pipeline)

Azurix was the collection entity of water operations:

Argentina (water)
Canada (water)
Mexico (water)
Wessex, England (water)
Brazil (electricity)
Korea (gas distribution)

Ms Mark was excellent at completing a deal. She was less good at buying at a price that facilitated making a profit. She too often neglected the political climate of the asset being acquired and its relevance for making future profits.

When the financial difficulties hit in October 2001, it was impossible to convert the international assets immediately into cash.

Other Difficulties

Enron had other difficult areas. Broadband in 2001 and Enron Energy Services were startups that were still losing money.

The New Power Company, an Enron startup, issued stock at $11 and the stock immediately climbed to $21. When that stock sank, Enron's inept attempts to avoid losses resulted in further accounting and financial problems.

Rhythms NetConnections was one of the Enron's successful (for a time) merchant assets. Enron made a $10 million investment in 1998. The stock went up from $21 to $69 and Enron's $10 million investment was worth $300 million. Fastow's LJM1 provided a "hedge". This was another of Enron's faulty hedges, a poor substitute for a real market driven hedge.

A Tragedy

On 25 January 2002, the dead body of J Clifford Baxter, a former Enron vice chairman, was found inside his Mercedes-Benz. He apparently committed suicide.

There is no reason to conclude that Mr Baxter had done anything inappropriate. He had left Enron in the Spring of 2001. There is reason to suspect that the Enron collapse was very upsetting to Mr Baxter.

The Extent of Corruption

Was Enron corrupt? How evil was the Enron management?

Let us leave out from consideration the shredding of documents by both Arthur Andersen and Enron when they knew investigations were pending. Also, leave out the amounts taken by Fastow and other employees from the several related entities. While upsetting, these actions were not the core elements of Enron's bankruptcy.

Consider the SPEs that were established or utilized for hedging purposes and the accounting for these entities (for example, Chewco and the Raptors). To a minor extent these were actually hedges (for small price changes of the hedged asset). The accounting and economic problems came into being when the losses became large.

It is interesting that the accounting for Chewco would have been technically acceptable (if not admirable) if an additional $7 million of independent equity had been raised. The failure to raise the $7 million is stupidity or carelessness, not corruption.

There were several other (maybe "many other") departures from good accounting. These were not consistent with the traditional objectives of financial accounting, but they did not necessarily indicate the existence of corruption.

It was desirable for Lay and Skilling to pay more attention to the accounting and financial details, but one can conject that they did not. Fastow was both too clever and not knowledgeable enough. He failed to consider the consequences of a severe fall in the value of the merchant assets and the value of the SPEs' assets. Fastow established a house of cards that could not withstand a slight breeze.

The auditors and the CFO of Enron did not keep the Board adequately informed. The investment banks and commercial banks helped to raise the capital necessary for Fastow to play his games. The Financial Accounting Standards Board failed to supply adequate consolidation rules. The SEC ruled that only 3% independent equity was necessary for nonconsolidation of a SPE. The Board allowed Fastow to administer a conflict of interest situation. History proved that was a mistake. Analysts oversold the Enron stock to the capital market and its stock price increased and then the management tried to prove that the analysts were correct. Instead, they proved that the analysts were wrong. There is plenty of blame to spread around, but aside from the possible exception of Fastow and his team, relatively little corruption.

Analysts recommended Enron stock after the investment banks knew that there were difficulties. This could be an illustration of the analysts bailing out the investment banks or it could be that the wall between investment banking and security analyses actually worked. Take your choice!

Sharing the Blame

Identifying the entities that can share in the blame for the Enron collapse results in a long list that includes:

1. Enron's top management and Board did not stop transactions that they did not understand (and maybe did not know about).
2. Investment banks and commercial banks, for not identifying the pitfalls for Enron associated with complexity and large amounts of leverage.
3. A law firm that seemed not to keep the Enron Board informed of all conflict of interest situations.
4. Rating agencies and security analysts that did not insist on better information.
5. The auditors seemed to be too permissive.
6. The CFO initiated many of the transactions that can be criticized.
7. Investors who paid too much for the stock (hindsight helps us with this one).
8. The designers of the accounting rules that facilitate the hiding of debt.

In 2002, Arthur Andersen was convicted in Federal Court of changing the wording of a report (they were not convicted of shredding of Enron records). The conviction was overturned. Michael J Kopper, a former mid-level Enron finance executive, in August 2002, pleaded guilty to conspiracy to commit wire fraud and money laundering. Kopper was involved with (as investor and manager) the SPEs, Chewco and LJM. One can conject that the federal government had Andrew Fastow in its sights and hit Kopper. A financial economist might find it difficult to understand how Kopper could be guilty of wire fraud and money laundering as a result of investing in and managing SPEs that did business with Enron, but that is the business of lawyers, and not to be easily understood by laymen.

Conclusions

There are several lessons to be learned from the Enron debacle.

First and most importantly, a finance officer can be "too smart". Using clever financial and accounting devices that confuse analysts and investors might work for a short while, but when the system collapses the consequences are magnified. If Enron had reported its merchant investment losses to go with the firm's trading and operating profits, the market would have digested this information and Enron would have survived.

Any firm that is heavily dependent on short-term credit is vulnerable to bad news reports that shake the market's faith in its reports. The media can bring down a firm that needs short-term credit.

Enron did many transactions whose primary objective seemed to be to mislead the person evaluating its financial performance. All the accounting hedges were of this nature as well as many of the put purchase transactions with the SPEs. Unfortunately, these transactions then led to a faulty accounting (failure to consolidate three entities) and a loss of faith by the market in Enron's top management.

There are many reasons why a firm's management should "do right". First, it is the honorable and correct thing to do. Second, it is likely to maximize shareholder value. Enron, when it found it could not buy an economic hedge for its merchant assets, should have reported the gains and losses as they occurred. If it had done this simple and the correct thing the Enron Corporation would still be operating and growing.

Enron's stock price implicitly promised large and continuous profitable growth. Enron's actual business activities were not always profitable and they did not promise continuous growth. What do managers do when their stock is greatly overvalued? In the Enron case some of the managers tried to sustain the illusion of continuous profitable growth. Unfortunately, it was an illusion. The Enron stock price as of 1 January 2001 could not be justified by the revised accounting numbers.

Enron had 3000–4000 SPEs. Obviously, we can only describe the function of a handful of these SPEs.

There is a tendency to look at the Enron collapse as being an event from which significant generalizations and wisdoms can be learned. Thus RW Stevenson in *The New York Times* (17 February 2002, Sec. 4, p. 1) writes:

> Still, it is possible that Enron's downfall could lead to a reexamination of what kind of capitalism the country is most comfortable with.

The lessons from Enron are much more limited than redefining capitalism. There will always be people who push any system to the limit. It might at times be necessary to tinker with the accounting and financial systems. Now is our time. However, it is desirable to avoid overreacting to the wrongdoing of Fastow at Enron.

Chapter 13

The Indictment of Lay and Skilling

The basic charge (paragraph 5) was:

> 5. As detailed below, defendants KENNETH L. LAY
> ("LAY"), JEFFREY K. SKILLING ("SKILLING"), and
> their conspirators, engaged in a wide-ranging scheme to
> deceive the investing public, including Enron's sharehold-
> ers, the SEC, and others (the "Victims"), about the true
> performance of Enron's businesses by: (a) manipulating
> Enron's publicly reported financial results; and (b) mak-
> ing public statements and representations about Enron's
> financial performance and results that were false and mis-
> leading in that they did not fairly and accurately reflect
> Enron's actual financial condition and performance, and
> they omitted to disclose facts necessary to make those
> statements and representations fair and accurate.

Paragraph 16 included the following:

> Due to the efforts of LAY, SKILLING, and their conspir-
> ators, the financial appearance of Enron presented to the
> investing public concealed the true state of Enron. Enron's
> publicly reported financial results and filings and its public
> descriptions of itself, including in public statements made
> by and with the knowledge of LAY and SKILLING did

147

not truthfully present Enron's financial position, results from operations, and cash flow of the company and omitted facts necessary to make the disclosures and statements that were made truthful and not misleading.

When the bad news of August 2001 was made public, Lay studied alternatives (paragraph 21):

> During the last two weeks of August 2001 and the first week of September 2001, LAY was briefed by numerous Enron employees on Enron's mounting and undisclosed financial and operational problems, including several billion dollars of losses embedded in Enron's assets and business units. As a result of these and other issues confronting Enron, LAY and Causey privately considered a range of potential solutions, including mergers, restructurings, and even divestiture of Enron's pipelines, assets that LAY considered to be the crown jewels of the company.

In the indictment, this is made to sound like a crime but is a normal reaction to financial challenges.

Paragraph 22 contains the statement:

> Among other things, as LAY knew, the total amount of losses embedded in Enron's assets and business units was, at a minimum, $7 billion.

Lay did not "know" this. The evidence as to the amount of losses was less than clear.

The specific acts that Lay and Skilling were accused of are (paragraph 26):

- Structuring financial transactions in a misleading manner in order to achieve earnings and cash flow objectives, avoid booking large losses in asset values, and conceal debt, including through the fraudulent use of purported third-party entities that in fact were not independent from Enron;

- Manufacturing earnings and artificially improving Enron's balance sheet through fraudulent overvaluation of assets;
- Fraudulently circumventing accounting standards applicable to the sale of financial assets in order to conceal the amount of Enron's debt and to create the false appearance of greater earnings and cash flow;
- Concealing large losses and failures in Enron's two highly-touted new businesses, Enron Broadband Services ("EBS") and EES;
- Manipulating earnings through fraudulent use of reserve accounts to mask volatility in Enron's wholesale energy trading earnings and use those reserves later in order to appear to achieve budget targets;
- Fraudulently circumventing accounting standards applicable to the disclosure and recognition of impairments to goodwill; and
- Making false and misleading statements, and omissions of facts necessary to make statements not misleading, about Enron's financial condition.

Paragraph 43 describes efforts by Enron to hide the magnitude of the EBS failure (EBS or Enron Broadband).

Paragraphs 44–47 allege improper use of accounting reserves. For example, paragraph 47 states:

> SKILLING and Causey fraudulently used funds that had been improperly placed in the 'Schedule C' reserve accounts to avoid reporting large losses in other areas of Enron's business. In the first quarter of 2001, SKILLING and Causey improperly used hundreds of millions of dollars of 'Schedule C' reserves to conceal from the investing public hundreds of millions of dollars in losses within Enron's EES business unit.

Of course, Skilling and Causey did not "fraudulently use funds" since there were no funds set aside. These were merely accounting entries and their description should reflect them.

Paragraph 48 alleges that Lay and Causey "fraudulently circumvented the accounting standards with respect to 'goodwill' ". This criminal act is illustrated using Wessex Water Services. The testimony regarding this issue was conflicting.

On 16 October 2001, Enron held a quarterly conference call with security analysts. Enron

> ... had suffered large losses, totaling approximately $1 billion ... these areas included many declining assets that had been concealed in the 'Raptor' hedges... However, LAY attempted to mislead the investing public and omit information about these losses in order to minimize the negative effect on Enron's stock price. LAY described the losses as 'nonrecurring', that is, a one-time or unusual earnings event. However, as LAY knew, the losses were not properly characterized as nonrecurring.

Since the $1 billion losses were related to merchant asset losses, they were in a sense nonrecurring. Their value could not go negative, without further decisions.

The 51 Counts

There were 51 counts of criminal charges. Obviously, the above brief excerpts are illustrative, but are not completely descriptive of the Government's case against Lay and Skilling.

The jury had a gigantic job since sensible arguments could be made for and against each of the criminal charges.

Too frequently, the jury had to determine the intent behind a statement. For example, when in the fall of 2001 Lay said he was optimistic about the future of Enron, was he lying or was he merely being the enthusiastic manager that he had been for so many years?

Reference

United States of America v. Jeffrey K. Skilling and Kenneth L. Lay, Defendents. United States District Court, Southern District of Texes, Houston, Division, Cr. No. N-04-25 (S-2).

Chapter 14

The Trial

The instructions of Judge Lake included the following (pp. 17652–17653):

> Good faith is a complete defense to the charges of conspiracy, securities fraud, and wire fraud contained in the indictment since good faith on the part of a Defendant is inconsistent with the intent to defraud or willfulness, which is an essential part of the charges.
>
> The burden of proof is not on the Defendants to prove their good faith since they have no burden to prove anything. The Government must establish beyond a reasonable doubt that the Defendants acted with specific intent to defraud as charged in the indictment.
>
> One who expresses an opinion honestly held by him or a belief honestly entertained by him is not chargeable with fraudulent intent even though his opinion is erroneous or his belief is mistaken. And similarly, evidence that establishes only that a person made a mistake in judgment or an error in management or was careless does not establish fraudulent intent.

This charge sets a high hurdle for the US Government to achieve a guilty verdict on the counts charged. "Fraudulent intent" is difficult to prove.

The Judge's charge goes on for 46 pages. I am sure that the jury needed a large amount of directions. While the Judge wrote in a direct simplified manner, all sorts of questions and qualifications must have occurred to the jurors as they discussed each count. This was a very difficult case for the jurors to determine the extent of guilt.

US Attorney Sean Berkowitz accused the defense with using the following theory (p. 18248):

> I went online last night and found a quote from a case. 'There's a theory that I heard about when I was in law school and lawyers know this theory, that if the law is against you, you attack the facts and if the facts are against you, you attack the other party'. That's the strategy.

Unfortunately, the theory also applies to elements of the Government's case.

Mr Berkowitz also departed from the relevant facts in order to argue for a conviction (pp. 18243–18244):

> Let's not forget that Enron went bankrupt when we're considering the credibility of these people, all right? This was the seventh largest company in the country, and it went bankrupt in a matter of months.

And why did Enron go bankrupt?

> And I submit to you, ladies and gentlemen, that the *Wall Street Journal* didn't report in October of 2001 that Andy Fastow was committing any crimes. All it did was talk about LJM and the relationship.

But, LJM was a part of Fastow's criminal activity.

Again, lacking a "smoking gun," Mr Berkowitz requested a leap of judgment (p. 18246):

> Mr Skilling and Mr Lay took that stand, and you should judge their demeanor, ladies and gentlemen. I would suggest to you that they were evasive, they denied clear documents, and they couldn't recall key issues. Together, the

both of them, over 200 times couldn't recall key issues, ladies and gentlemen. You saw them fight and struggle with even the simplest questions. You can judge their credibility just like you judge the cooperators' credibility.

Again, to prove that Skilling committed a crime, consider (p. 18214):

> This is to Mr Skilling. 'Intense pressure to close deals driven by earnings considerations has motivated Enron to assume extraordinary investment risks or risks which have not been appropriately priced'. That's what they were doing, ladies and gentlemen. They desperately needed LJM in order to hit their earnings targets in 1999 and the first part of 2000 before the California volatility started kicking up.

But nothing in this paragraph implies a criminal act. Consider the following (p. 18264):

> that Mr Skilling said, 'Let's go for it'. And you heard from Mr Fastow. 'It was there to help manage earnings'.

"Let us go for it" is not a criminal act.

US Attorney Ms K Ruemmler shifted the focus from the crimes of Skilling and Lay to the costs of the Enron bankruptcy on the small investor:

> You heard a lot about this speech that was given by the SEC Chairman Levitt. You've seen it from time to time in this trial. He described who the average American investors are. It's the single mother saving for her child's education; a man who has worked at a company for 20 years saving for his retirement; people like Johnny Nelson, John Sides, and Patty Klien who came in here and testified in this trial; people who believed and relied on what these two men said; people who mistakenly placed their trust in these two men.

You will recall Mr Nelson came in, the man who worked in New Mexico, and he said, 'Ken Lay broke my trust'. These people relied on the accuracy and the integrity and the fullness and completeness of the information being given by the CEOs of the company. They had every right to believe that the numbers that the company was putting out were not being propped up by accounting gimmicks and trickery.

Ms Ruemmler is confusing the attempts by Lay to save Enron with the factors that led to bankruptcy. But these are strong arguments for convicting Skilling and Lay of something.

The owners of Enron were cheated. They were stolen from. They were profoundly harmed by what these two men did, ladies and gentlemen. That is a fraud. That is why we are here. That is why this matters.

It is unfortunate when investors lose as a result of a company's financial difficulties. But it is not necessarily a fraud. Describe the fraud not the consequences of bad business decisions.

Ms Ruemmler falls back to the testimony of witnesses who the Government has promised reduced jail terms (p. 17700):

Witness after witness after witness came into this courtroom, ladies and gentlemen, and they said, 'I lied. We lied. I stole. We stole. I committed fraud. We committed fraud'. These people, Ben Glisan, Dave Delainey, Wes Colwell, Ken Rice, Kevin Hannon, Mark Koenig, Paula Rieker, some of the most senior executives at Enron, came in and told you that. 'I lied. We lied. I stole. We stole'.

But the paragraph does not include a quote that Lay or Skilling lied or stole.

Kathryn Ruemmler also made a large deal of Lay's statement "Rules are important but you shouldn't be a slave to the rules". Ms Ruemmler went on to say "That says it all. Mr Lay, Mr Skilling, and his lieutenants were so arrogant they did not think the rules applied to them". Is the conclusion that one should be a slave to rules? An innocent management recommendation is changed into a mandate by Lay to break all rules. This is not good thinking but it is an effective distortion to present to a jury.

She also cited Skilling's resignation in August as a proof that "Enron as a corporation was financially beat". Not proof but maybe a hint.

Ms Ruemmler wants to show criminal intent so she refers first to the Raptors (p. 17707):

> What's the cover story? The cover story is that, well, these were all approved by Arthur Andersen, by lawyers. You saw, you have them in evidence, thousands, I think, pages of documents to make the Raptors look legit. They were just typical financing structures. Mr Lay told investors that they were so insignificant that he wasn't even sure that they had a name.

The cover story is pretty good for Skilling and Lay. Not good for Fastow and the other accounting-finance people.

As I am extracting from Ms Ruemmler's arguments, I am not being completely fair. To be perfectly fair, I would have to include Ms Ruemmler's complete unedited (by me) arguments. So understand, these are selected excerpts and they are not attempts to prove the innocence or guilt of Skilling or Lay. They do tend to show that unfair statements were made by the US Attorneys.

The Charges

There were initially seven counts against Lay and 31 counts against Skilling. These were later reduced to six and 28 counts. The Enron prosecutors asked that two counts of securities fraud and one count of making false statements to auditors by Skilling be dismissed. This left 28 counts of fraud, conspiracy, and insider trading. For Lay, the judge dismissed one count of securities fraud (an analyst/conference call on 12 November 2001). This left six counts of fraud and conspiracy.

Mark to Market Accounting

In 1991, Skilling convinced Ken Lay and other top Enron managers that the company should shift from cost-based to mark to market accounting. He then convinced Arthur Andersen and the SEC that the change was appropriate. The change would prove to be very significant to Skilling in ways that he did not anticipate. But first an explanation of two accounting alternatives.

Assume a company buys a share of stock for $50. The stock goes up to $90. Using cost-based accounting, no entry is made for the value change. Most significantly, no income is recognized.

Now assume the firm uses mark to market accounting. There is recorded $40 of income and the asset is recorded at $90. In this example, it is clear that mark to market is a superior accounting method compared to cost-based. But the world is more complex than the simple stock example with a well-defined market price.

Now assume that the firm has engaged in trading gas contracts. It has sold an obligation to supply gas for the next ten years. It has also bought a contract to buy gas for the next five years. The firm has two choices applying mark to market accounting. It can compute the net present value of the two contracts for five years (even though the contract to supply gas has a life of ten years). Or it can estimate the cost of obtaining gas for years 6–10 and compute the net present value of ten years.

Obviously, a large amount of judgment enters into mark to market accounting. From 1991 to 2001, Enron used this method of accounting for a wide range of complex accounting transactions. There was very little valid criticism to the way that Enron and Arthur Andersen applied the accounting method. One could object to the way that Enron estimated future incomes using estimated prices, or to the use of reserves that were established in case future prices were not equal to the expected prices, but there were not obvious attempts to manipulate Enron's incomes from 1991 to 2001 using mark to market accounting.

Mark to market accounting used aggressively by Enron when there were not clearly defined market prices was a distortion of mark to market accounting in theory. The theory said that when there were well-defined market prices (as with the prices of the stock traded on the New York Stock Exchange), mark to market beat cost-based accounting. When future market prices had to be estimated, then support for mark to market dropped off significantly (or disappeared).

Assume Ford Motor Company has just completed a new auto assembly plant at a cost of $500,000,000 and with a net present value of $900,000,000. Should the $900,000,000 be recorded as income immediately? Accounting practice says no to recording the NPV of $900,000,000 saying that the income must be realized through time. But practice did allow Enron to record income on trading contracts immediately even though the uncertain cash flows will only be realized in the future.

Interestingly, the US Government grabbed mark to market as a means of showing that Skilling did not honestly report asset values and shows losses as soon as they could be estimated. For example, with EES as an example, Ms Ruemmler states (p. 17724):

> Ladies and gentlemen, Ms Curry's testimony and Mr Delainey's testimony flatly contradict that. You cannot — these are losses. They specifically described them. You got the document in evidence. They were errors, errors in the contracts. They are losses. You can't just say, 'We're going to renegotiate them out later'. In mark-to-market accounting, as Ms Curry, who was the accountant, told you, the losses needed to be booked immediately. ...
>
> Ms Curry: 'The 250 million should have been booked in the first quarter'. Dave Delainey: 'The 100 to 150 was an immediate issue'. Jeff Skilling: 'We can just renegotiate these out of the normal process'. You can't do that. That's fraud. There's no nice way to put it. It's accounting fraud. You find errors in your contract, you have to book it.

But if Skilling thought the losses could be avoided, then not recording the loss was reasonable. You can disagree but that does not result in Skilling committing a crime.

And then Ms Ruemmler moves on to California (p. 17726):

> What happens on the 27th? Something significant. The California Public Utility Commission issues a surcharge. Immediate loss to EES. We're now three days to the end of the quarter. What can you do? ...
>
> The other documents show — we'll talk about those in a second — that Enron took a reserve for this $225 million loss that Mr Delainey talked about.

It is not obvious that Ms Ruemmler has made a correct statement. If Enron "took a reserve" means that Enron set up a reserve, then the debit was to an expense account and Enron did the right thing.

There is also the issue of the value of Enron's international assets. Note that goodwill accounting is a variant of mark to market accounting. If the goodwill value recorded on the firm's book cannot be supported by the estimates of cash flows and their present value, then the goodwill asset amount should be reduced. Ms Ruemmler states that Enron had overstated its assets (p. 17800):

> Mr Skilling himself had presented to the board that Enron's international assets were overvalued by his own estimate of about $4.5 billion.
>
> Mr Skilling testified that he viewed these as sort of his own view of a fire-sale price and that he was recommending to the board and Mr Lay that they not sell the international assets at this time.

Remember Skilling was not a fan of Ms Mark and would not overstate the value of the international assets (purchased by Mark for Enron).

Mr K Hannon had taken over international asset management. His testimony was as follows (a conversation with Lay on 15 August 2001) (p. 17801). The questions asked by Ms Ruemmler are

'Did you have a plan that had been developed at Enron regarding potential write-downs because of something known as a goodwill accounting change?'

'Yes'.

'What was the plan?'

'To take a $2 billiion write-down associated with the goodwill for international assets'.

You recall, again, without getting into the minutia of the goodwill accounting rules, all it says is that, if you had — if there's a determination that there's an overvaluation, you have to take a loss, put simply.

Mark to market accounting is a two-edged sword. Assets have to be written down as well as up. Unfortunately, there is not always agreement the decrease in value has occurred (p. 17820):

'A final decision has been made that we are not willing to take any goodwill impairment on Wessex'.

Who made that final decision? Mr Lay made it.

We do not know that Wessex's goodwill was impaired in August 2001. But, we do know that Enron (Ms Mark) paid a large premium for Wessex and it could be argued that the goodwill was impaired the day that Wessex was acquired by Enron.

Mr Sean Berkowitz, a US Attorney, is also enthusiastic about applying mark to market accounting (p. 18301):

'Critical period of time. Avoid a goodwill write-down. Third quarter'. Wessex. Skilling's estimate. Remember that chart? $2 billion in fair value. Book value, 3 billion. September 27th e-mail from the Azurix chief financial officer. 'Decision has been made not willing to take any goodwill impairment on Wessex'. ...

Elektro was another asset, ladies and gentlemen. 'Elektro is troubled', finance committee, June, 2001; 'Elektro is troubled', September, 2001. 'Analyst call, Elektro is not

a bad asset, it's a good asset', the time they need to avoid
a goodwill write-down.

Do we want to consider the judgment that an asset has not declined
in value a crime?

Understand that with mark to market accounting, large amounts
of income can be recorded (the value of contracts in excess of their
cost) but there may not be a dollar of cash. This is not necessarily
evil. Consider a stock bought at $100 and now worth (traded on a
broad market) at $1,000,000. There is really $999,900 of income even
though until sale there is no cash received.

If an element of uncertainty is introduced, then we begin to be
uneasy about the accuracy of saying there is $999,900 of income in
the above example. Knowing (revealing) the extent of uncertainty is
crucial to having a good accounting (reporting) system.

Michael Ramey

In March 2006, Michael W Ramey, Lay's lead attorney, as he cross-
examined Andrew Fastow, suffered discomfort that was later diag-
nosed as a heart attack. He then missed more than a month of the
trial. His absence most likely had an enormous effect on the trial's
outcome.

The Testimony of Lay

We should not underestimate the importance of the way that Ken Lay
acted as he gave testimony. Everyone expected him to be his usual
charming gracious person. McLean and Elkind (*Fortune*, 15 May
2006, p. 72) state, "But he seemed unable to get past his indignant
self-righteousness, his sense that he was simply too good a man to
ever have to answer questions about his role in Enron's bankruptcy".

When asked in the witness stand to name one mistake he had made
when managing Enron, Lay replied "approving the hiring of Andrew
Fastow and, of course, promoting him to chief financial officer". It is

difficult to imagine a second CFO who could have placed Enron in bankruptcy in the year 2006.

Skilling

Berkowitz had several issues with Skilling including:

a. Why did he leave Enron in August 2001?
b. The source of Enron profits (speculative and volatile trading)?
c. The $200 million accounting charge (which of Enron's units should be charged?). Should Enron Energy Systems (EES) be charged?
d. The magnitude of Enron's trading risks (see b above).

None of these issues seemed to deserve extended jail time, even if the Government positions were correct.

Mr Skilling testified (18 April 2006) that "Did I ever give anyone any instruction to change the results of the quarter? I did not". The Government did not prove that he was not telling the truth. He had said "shoot for 34" when told they were going to hit 32.

Skilling testified that in August 2001, the financial affairs of Enron were so strong, fraud was not necessary, in fact, would be nonsensical.

The *New York Times* (Alexi Barrionuero, 21 April 2006) wrote "This was a man who did not like to be questioned, to be told he was wrong, to be asked, even, just to listen".

Berkowitz made a lot of Skilling's investment in a photo company headed by Jennifer Binder, a woman he dated and with which Enron did business. Was this event relevant?

Demeanor

Both Skilling and Lay did not project pure innocence when they testified. Thus, Ms Ruemmler asks the jury to remember this (p. 17701):

> So I would ask you to think back — as you're listening to those arguments, think back about the demeanor of those witnesses. Did they make every effort to answer questions in a forthright manner? Did they offer excuses for their

conduct? Did they attempt to shift responsibility onto others, the *Wall Street Journal*, the press, the government, the Enron Task Force? Did they attempt to shift responsibility from themselves? Ask yourselves that. ...

On cross examination, both Mr Lay and Mr Skilling fought, argued, made long speeches, evaded questions. They both at various times told Mr Berkowitz and Mr Hueston, 'You just don't get it. You don't understand.

Mr Berkowitz also directed the jury to consider demeanor (p. 18246):

> Mr Skilling and Mr Lay took that stand, and you should judge their demeanor, ladies and gentlemen. I would suggest to you that they were evasive, they denied clear documents, and they couldn't recall key issues. Together, the both of them, over 200 times couldn't recall key issues, ladies and gentlemen. You saw them fight and struggle with even the simplest questions. You can judge their credibility just like you judge the cooperators' credibility.

One of the simple questions Lay could not remember concerned the anonymous August letter he received, but if the question had made clear that the letter was from Ms Watkins, there would have been no problem. Not all the questions were clearly put forth.

Testimony

In testimony on 2nd March, Kevin P Hannon (chief operating officer of broadband) stated that Skilling stated "They're on to us". The implication was that *Wall Street* analysts were beginning to understand Enron. While a strange comment, it does not translate "They have caught us doing criminal acts". However, this comment's importance was stressed by the US Attorneys. David W Delainey (head of Enron Energy Services, EES) testified that the Raptors were "a pot of money we used to manipulate our income statement." That is not accurate. The Raptors sold puts to Enron and to the extent that they were valid puts they protected Enron from possible losses from merchant asset value declines.

Ben F Glisan, Enron's Treasurer, helped Fastow develop the Raptors and in September 2003 pled guilty to conspiracy. The Raptors were part of the charge (manipulating income).

The Duration

There were 53 days of trial and 51 witnesses and four weeks of testimony by Lay and Skilling. Several important individuals did not testify including David B Duncan who was a lead auditor of the Arthur Andersen team that audited Enron. Seven witnesses for the government who pled guilty to Enron-related crimes and three others were granted immunity relative to testimony given.

An Observation

The *Wall Street Journal* (31 May 2006, author James B Stewart) gave the annual award for "worst white-collar defense of the year" to Skilling and Lay. "Mr Skilling seemed at times evasive, confused, and inconsistent". Mr Lay "undermined his own reputation as a benevolent civic leader in minutes, alternately displaying arrogance and self-righteousness. Mr Lay even grew testy while being questioned by his own lawyer ..."

The Judge's Charge to Jury

The Honorable Sim Lake (the Judge of the Skilling–Lay trial) in his charge to the jury stated (p. 17682):

> "To establish that Mr Skilling sold Enron stock on the basis of the material, non-public information, the Government must prove beyond a reasonable doubt that he used the material, non-public information in making his decision to sell Enron stock".

Skilling made his first significant sale of Enron stock on 17 September 2001. He sold 500,000 shares (grossing $15 million) (page 17696 of the trial).

But the US Attorney (Ms K.H. Ruemmler) also claims that Skilling knew that Enron was in trouble long before 17 September 2001 (p. 17693):

> On that day, August 14th of 2001, Jeff Skilling and Ken Lay told Enron's investors and employees that the company was in the strongest and best financial shape that it had ever been in. It wasn't. That wasn't true, and they knew that. Approximately three months later, after this critical day, Enron collapsed.

Insider Information

Ms Ruemmler claims that Skilling and Lay knew Enron was in trouble for at least 2 years (p. 17693):

> What did Mr Skilling and Mr Lay know on August 14th of 2001? You've heard a lot of testimony about this in the trial, ladies and gentlemen. Two of Enron's touted growth businesses, EES and EBS, had failed. They cost the company — those two businesses had cost the company a ton of money. Over the prior two years, the performance of those businesses had been systematically covered up through accounting tricks and misleading statements.

If Skilling knew Enron was sick, why did he wait until the middle of September 2001 to sell a portion of his holdings? Ms Ruemmler states (p. 17770):

> Earnings manipulation, accounting trickery, fraud. Fourth quarter 1999, it was done. Second quarter of 2000, it was done. Mr Delainey told you that this was standard operating procedure at Enron.

Obviously, with insider information, Skilling and Lay should have started selling Enron shares by at least 1999.

Skilling's Departure

Mr Sean Berkowitz, in the Government's rebuttal argument in reference to Skilling's departure from Enron in August 2001 and his attempt to return in September 2001, said the following (p. 18251):

> He talks about coming back to the company, ladies and gentlemen. Let me ask you this. I've got two better questions: One, why did he leave? You saw the 11 reasons he gave. Do you know why Mr Skilling left the company? Did they answer that question? Here's a better question: Why didn't they want him back? Ask yourselves that, ladies and gentlemen, when you're considering Mr Skilling offering to come back and they said a resounding 'No'.

There is one answer to both of the Berkowitz's questions. Skilling was falling apart and he knew it thus his resignation as Enron President. Also, his colleagues and Ken Lay knew he was in trouble thus he could not rescue Enron in September. Read McLean and Elkind (2003, pp. 325–326) for the Skilling–Grubman exchange during a conference call after the first quarter's earnings release. Pages 337–339 continues the tale of Skilling's mental decline. He obviously needed rest from Enron's difficulties. It is unfair for Berkowitz to use Skilling's resignation and Enron's refusal to hire him back as implying that he should be convicted of a crime.

The Verdict

US District Judge, Sim Lake, instructed the jury to convict Lay and Skilling if the two men ignored crimes at Enron. They did not have to commit crimes.

Lay was convicted of six counts and Skilling of 28 counts.

On 23 October 2006, Skilling was sentenced to 24 years and four months in prison (Bernard Ebbers, CEO of World Com was sentenced to 25 years). He was convicted of 19 felony counts. Andrew Fastow received a sentence of six years (as a result of a plea bargain and of agreeing to testify). He was originally sentenced to ten years.

Judge Lake said "As the many victims have testified, his crimes have imposed on hundreds if not thousands a life sentence of proverty".

Of course, no evidence was presented that Skilling caused Enron's failure. Also, if the Government was correct, Skilling even committed crimes in order to improve the firm's financial status.

Almost all of Skillings $60 million assets will be seized by the Government ($45 million to the victims of investing in Enron, $15.5 million will go to Skilling's lawyers).

On 17 October 2006, Judge Lake vacated the conviction of Lay given his fatal heart attack on 5 July 2006.

Would there have been a Skilling–Lay trial if Enron's good assets had earned at least $2 billion a year for the years 2001 on? If there had been a trial, would either man had been found guilty?

Reference

McLean, B and P Elkind (2003). *The Smartest Guys in the Room: The Amazing Rise and Scandalous Fall of Enron.* New York, NY: Portfolio (the Penguin Group).

Chapter 15

A Slice of the Skilling–Lay Trial*

The Superseding Indictment (Grand Jury Charges) included the following statement (p. 26):

> Enron ... had committed a $1.2 billion accounting error...

First, I will explain the accounting issue and the financial significance of the error, then the disclosures by Enron, then reference the importance of this issue to the Skilling–Lay trial by citing the closing argument given at the trial.

The Accounting Issue

In 1985, the emerging issues task force studied the issue of classifying notes received for capital stock (see, the EITF Abstracts, 1989; SEC Staff Accounting Bulletin No. 40). The issue was whether an "enterprise should report the note receivable as a reduction of shareholders' equity or as an asset" (p. 95).

> The Task Force reached a consensus that reporting the note as an asset is generally not appropriate, except in very limited circumstances when there is substantial evidence of

*The author owes thanks to Don W Schnedeker, librarian of the Johnson School Library.

167

ability and intent to pay within a reasonably short period of time ...

The SEC requires that public companies report notes received in payment for the enterprise's stock as a deduction from shareholders' equity. Task Force members confirmed that the predominant practice is to offset the notes and stock in the equity section. However, such notes may be recorded as an asset if collected in cash prior to issuance of the financial statements.

The notes receivable is not an asset, but rather is a deduction from stockholders' equity. Unfortunately, this very exact conclusion was buried in EITF Abstracts Issue No. 85-1 (1985), and Enron and Arthur Andersen both got the accounting wrong in the year 2000. It was an easy error to make. It is very doubtful if either Skilling or Lay was aware of the correct accounting or even the incorrect accounting.

The Year 2000 Enron Annual Report

The year 2000 Enron Annual Report Footnote 16 (pp. 48–49) contained a description of the transaction but the issues are far from clear.

In 2000, Enron entered into transactions with the Related Party to hedge certain merchant investments and other assets. As part of the transactions, Enron (i) contributed to newly-formed entities (the Entities) assets valued at approximately $1.2 billion, including $150 million in Enron notes payable, 3.7 million restricted shares of outstanding Enron common stock and the right to receive up to 18.0 million shares of outstanding Enron common stock in March 2003 (subject to certain conditions) and (ii) transferred to the Entities assets valued at approximately $309 million, including a $50 million note payable and an investment in an entity that indirectly holds warrants convertible into common stock of an Enron equity method investee. In return, Enron received economic interests in the Entities. $309 million in notes receivable, of which $259 million is recorded at Enron's carryover basis of zero, and a special distribution from the Entities in the form of $1.2 billion in notes receivable, subject to changes in the principal for amounts payable by Enron in connection with the execution of additional derivative instruments.

The accounting error was made in the second quarter of 2000 and the first quarter of 2001 and carried forward into the second quarter of 2001.

Enron's Form 10-Q for Quarter Ending 30 September 2001

The 10-Q made clear the exact nature of the accounting error (pp. 18–19):

> As described in more detail below, four SPEs known as Raptor I-IV (collectively, Raptor) were created in 2000 to permit Enron to hedge market risk in certain of its investments. . . . As part of the capitalization of these entities, Enron issued common stock in exchange for a note receivable. Enron increased notes receivable and shareholders' equity to reflect this transaction. Enron now believes that, under generally accepted accounting principles, the note receivable should have been presented as a reduction to shareholders' equity (similar to a shareholder loan).

It should be noted that the accounting error did not affect the income or the cash flow of any time period.

Also, the total assets of Enron were $65 billion and the total equity was $11 billion so that $1.2 billion reduction in equity was not material from a financial analysis point of view.

Enron 8-K of 8 November 2001

The discussion of the $1.2 error was continued in the 8-K of 8 November 2001 (p. 2):

> The restatements discussed below affect prior periods. After taking into account Enron's previously disclosed $1.2 billion adjustment to shareholders' equity in the third quarter of 2001, these restatements have no effect on Enron's current financial position.

The specific adjustments to shareholders' equity are described (p. 5).

> As discussed in Section 3 below, concerning Enron's recent disclosure of a $1.2 billion reduction to shareholders' equity in the third quarter of 2001, shareholders' equity will be reduced by $172 million beginning as of June 30, 2000, and by an additional $828 million beginning as of March 31, 2001, to properly record notes receivable (described in Section 3 below) as a reduction to equity.

Enron 10-Q of 19 November 2001

This 10-Q describes in more detail the corrections made for the errors made in 2000 and the first quarter of 2001. The errors persisted through 30 June 2001.

Subjective Evaluation of Enron's Actions

Enron made accounting errors (the same error) during 2000 and the first quarter of 2001. The error was described in the third quarter of 2001 (10-Q of 30 September 2001), again described in Enron's 8-K of 8 November 2001, also in the 10-Q for the quarter ending 30 September 2001, and finally in the 8-K of 8 November 2001.

The explanations of the error made clear that it had no material effect on the financial evaluation of Enron's value. The original error and its correction did not affect Enron's earnings, cash flow, or liquidity measures. It was a pure accounting error made, explained in detail, and corrected by Enron and Arthur Andersen.

It is possible that either or both Skilling and Lay knew the original error, but very unlikely given the technical nature (a rare accounting pecularity) of the error. In any event, as soon as the error was uncovered by Arthur Andersen, it received adequate publicity by Enron setting the accounting record straight. Certainly, there was no evidence of criminal intent on the part of Skilling and Lay, but consider the following references.

The Trial

Ms Kathryn H Ruemmler stated in her closing arguments (for the prosecution):

> A large accounting error is discovered with the Raptors during this time. It's going to result in a $1.2 billion equity reduction. The Company is going to have to take massive write-downs because of the Raptor problems and these new goodwill accounting rules.

The lawyer connects an independent $1.2 billion write-down with two other independent events (pp. 17694–17695). We have to assume that the prosecution did not want to waste a $1.2 billion innocent error so they connected it to the Raptors which were very much subject to valid criticism.

Now, consider the rebuttal arguments of US Attorney Mr Sean Berkowitz (pp. 18302–18304).

> This is the $1.2 billion accounting error that they found out about at the end of August. . . .
>
> They didn't want to call it, as Mr Glisan told you, an accounting error because, if they did that, if they called it an accounting error, ladies and gentlemen, they'd have to do a restatement, if that's what it was called. So what did they do? They decided to try and bury the disclosure in

> a call, not in the earnings release, and say that it was in
> connection with the unwind of the Raptors. It's all normal.
> There's nothing unusual about it.
>
> They tried to mislead the market about this, ladies and
> gentlemen, but it's not true. It was — he makes the rep-
> resentation that it was in connection with the unwind of
> the Raptors.

First, the error had nothing to do with earnings. To release it in
an earnings release would be completely inappropriate. Second, as
referenced above, the 10-Q's and the 8-K's released by Enron made
it clear that there was $1.2 billion accounting error. There was no
attempt to hide the nature of the $1.2 correction.

Berkowitz does not stop with the above misleading comments
(p. 18304):

> It couldn't have been in connection with the Raptor
> unwind. The only reason to do that is to try and minimize.
> And why is he minimizing? Because Mr Skilling had just
> left. Enron was under incredible pressure. He had already
> promised there was no other shoe to drop. They had been
> criticized for aggressive and black box accounting, and an
> accounting error would have caused a restatement, and it
> would have been game over.
>
> The public was entitled to know, and he — you heard
> Ms Rieker, Mr Koenig, and Mr Glisan all talk about this
> decision to conceal. That's Count 28 as well, ladies and
> gentlemen.

Berkowitz has to know that Enron, as of August 2001, is going
to have to restate its income statements of the past several years for
real errors in income measurement not the irrelevant $1.2 reduction
in stock equity because it should not have been increased in the first
place.

If the $1.2 billion accounting error and Lay's reaction to it is all
the Government has as evidence, the verdict on Count 28 should be
innocent.

Conclusions

It is not too difficult to imagine a situation where a group of Government lawyers concluded that Skilling and Lay were guilty of many criminal acts and that a moral and ethical position is to try to convict using fair means or less than fair means. Unfortunately, they chose an event (an accounting error by Enron) that is a very bad foundation for concluding that Skilling and Lay had criminal intent in their actions concerning this transaction.

Obviously, the Government's case against Lay and Skilling went far beyond the one accounting error. Unfortunately, the same pattern of errors and exaggerations appear in other arguments.

The objective of the lawyers representing the US Government should be to facilitate justice and not to obtain a verdict of guilty using not quite accurate statements, especially when not quite accurate statements by the accused is the crime for which individuals are being charged.

References

EITF Abstracts (1989). FASB, Norwalk, CT.

Enron Annual Report (2000).

Enron's Form 10-Q for Quarter Ending 30 September 2001.

Enron's Form 8-K of 8 November 2001.

Enron's Form 10-Q for Quarter Ending 19 November 2001.

SEC Staff Accounting Bulletin No. 40, Topic 4-E, "Receivables from Sale of Stock".

Transcript of Proceedings Before the Honorable Sim Lake and a Jury, United States of America vs. Jeffrey K Skilling and Kenneth L Lay.

United States of America vs. Jeffrey K Skilling and Kenneth L Lay, *Superseding Indictment*, Cr. No. H-04-25 (S-2) United States District Court, Southern District of Texas, Houston Division, p. 26.

Chapter 16

The Skilling–Lay Trial: Fair or Foul?

This chapter will review selected testimony and concluding comments regarding Enron's alleged management of earnings made during the Skilling–Lay trial (2006). First, we will briefly review the academic accounting literature and then summarize the concluding comments made by the US Attorneys.

It is important to note that the objective of this chapter is not to confirm the guilt or innocence of Skilling or Lay. That would require more legal expertise and information than the author possesses. The objective is much more limited. It is to suggest that frequently in the trial complex accounting issues were excessively simplified or incorrectly analyzed in order to make a legal point not justified by the accounting evidence.

Earnings Management: Academic Literature

Ayers *et al.* (2006) find that (p. 651), "Consistent with earnings management, results suggest that the association between discretionary accruals and earning intensifies around the profit benchmark". The closer the actual results are to the target, the more likely the firm will use discretionary accruals to achieve the target. The authors cite 22 other papers that deal with earnings management.

Ewert and Wagenhofer (2005) examine whether tightening accounting standards reduces earnings management. They find (p. 1113),

> That real earnings management increases with tighter accounting standards is a subtle consequence of higher relevance of reported earnings, which increases the marginal benefit of earnings management.

The authors cite 21 papers of which 17 deal with earnings management.

We could include the conclusions of numerous other published papers but we will restrict our discussion to the above two papers and reach the following conclusions:

1. The issue of earnings management has been extensively studied.
2. Earnings management is not rare but rather is very extensive.
3. The efforts of managers to influence the accounting earnings have not led to an extensive series of criminal court cases unless there is significant fraud.

The Indictment

Consider the following statement (p. 22 of the Indictment):

> In fact, as Skilling knew Enron reaped huge profits in 2000 from energy trading in California and concealed hundred of millions of dollars of those earnings in undisclosed reserve accounts. As Skilling also knew, by late January 2001, California utilities owed EES hundreds of millions of dollars that EES could not collect, and Enron personnel had concealed large reserves that Enron was forced to use to offset those uncollectible receivables within Enron Wholesale's books.

On p. 23 of the Indictment we have:

> EES was owed hundreds of millions of dollars in receivables by California utilities that it could not collect and that Enron personnel were concealing within Enron Wholesale.

The first sentence says that Enron made hundred of millions of dollars, but hid these earnings in reserve accounts and thus understated earnings. This alleged hiding of earnings would most likely be achieved by debiting an expense account and crediting a reserve for uncollectibles. This would result in less earnings than if the entry was not made by recording the expense and the reserve. If this entry was not appropriate, earnings would be understated.

The second sentence starting with "As Skilling also knew ..." that there were "hundreds of millions of dollars that EES could not collect..." This implies that Enron should have set up a large "reserve for uncollectibles" which the first sentence says that they did set up, but implies they should not have.

Together, the two sentences state that Enron's accounting was more or less correct (we do not know what the exact numbers should have been).

On p. 23 of the Indictment, reference is again made to receivables that Enron could not collect "and that Enron personnel were concealing within Enron wholesale". But setting up reserves for uncollectibles was appropriate, not a concealment. There might be faulty accounting for reserves by Enron, but the indictment does not clearly identify it.

The Concluding Comments of US Attorneys

Ms K. Ruemmler was a US Attorney in the Skilling–Lay trial. She established that "at Enron it was critically important for Enron to meet its earning targets" (p. 17714). If the targets were not met, "Stock price would go down". Unfortunately for the prosecution, these statements and other similar statements, apply to nearly every company listed in the New York Stock Exchange. Was there more pressure at Enron than at other companies? We do not know.

There is a quote (attributed to Skilling),

> We have to try to get the P/E multiple up (p. 17715).

This is a standard goal of CEOs and not a crime.

A finance officer tells the Enron Board in December of 2000 that the EES business is worth $15 a share. In January 2001, Skilling tells investors that EES (retail business) will be worth $23 a share (p. 17718). Ms Ruemmler states (p. 17719), "That $23 a share is the motive for why EES failed". This, of course, makes little sense. Maybe the transcript is wrong, but EES did not fail because Skilling said it was worth $23 a share.

Ms Ruemmler states, "you can convict Mr Lay and Mr Skilling of conspiracy to commit securities fraud and Mr Skilling of all of the counts relating to EES ..."

It would appear that one could be critical of the execution of EES's function (pp. 17721–17722). But that does not mean that the business of delivering electricity did not have value.

Ruemmler reports a meeting with Skilling, Delainey, and others to discuss a reorganization with accounting consequences. Skilling states, "What do you want to do?" (p. 17727) and Delainey concludes that this was an order, "Get in line". It is too large a leap to go from Skilling's "What do you want to do?" to "Get in line".

Ms Ruemmler established that "Meeting the consensus estimate" (p. 17761) was a widespread practice. Enron was not unique having this objective. On p. 17762,

> the investing public was never told that Enron could pull
> a penny here, pull a penny there, for purposes of meeting
> the consensus estimate ... because it's fraud.

Maybe it was fraud, or maybe there were other explanations for adjustment of the income statements.

Ms Rieker "talking about managing that consensus estimate, getting the analysts where they need to be. ..." This is not fraud if it is rather working to have the analysts' estimates be reasonable and achievable.

Ms Ruemmler says (p. 17765) "That's fraud". Meeting the $0.31 estimate is not a fraud. The method used to achieve the $0.31 could be fraud, but p. 17765 and other pages of her concluding comments do not tell how the $0.31 was achieved. "Mr Skilling wanted to beat *The Street* by two cents instead of one" (p. 17768). But did he direct anyone to do something that was criminal?

"How could the numbers be coming in hot?" (p. 17769). The answer is that the numbers could be hot or cold or something in between. We do not know until we see them and analyze them.

On pages 17772–17773, there is a discussion about the use of accounting reserves. There are situations where not using reserves is faulty accounting. Consider a $100,000,000 accounts receivable but there is a significant probability that the entire amount will not be collected. A reserve for uncollectible should be established. But the exact amount of uncollectibles is an estimate. Ms Ruemmler states (p. 17773) "how do you know that the reserve actually reflect the true financial results of the company?" The fact is that the "true financial results" are not known even after the fact, but only estimates are known. To hope for truth in accounting is being excessively optimistic.

Can accounting for reserves be misused? Yes. Did Enron misuse reserve accounting? Yes, if the entries to the reserve accounts were used solely to achieve earnings objectives. The statement by Skillings (p. 17776) "You have a billion dollars or so in reserves as a head start". Does not clearly indicate fraud.

LJM is a conflict of interest problem (p. 17778). It is not accounting fraud. How much time did Skilling spend on LJM? (p. 17779). Skilling says very little. Ms Ruemmler says he spent a lot. If he had spent a lot of time, we would hope LJM would have been folded before it started to operate.

Conclusions

One of the classic method to manipulate earnings is to use reserve accounts. However, a reserve for uncollectibles (or allowance for uncollectibles) is a generally accepted use of reserves. The reserves can turn out to be too large or too small and still be good honest accounting at the time they are created. Instead of uncollectibles a reserve account can be used to estimate any ill-defined expense and liability. Because the actual amount is different than the estimate, does not mean that there is fraud.

Accounting is an art and not an exact science. The use of a reserve account should be carefully controlled and analyzed, but a difference between the original estimate and the final amount deemed to be appropriate does not, by itself, prove that fraud has been committed.

References

Ayers, BC, J Jiang and PE Yeung (2006). Discretionary accruals and earnings management: An analysis of pseudo earnings targets. *The Accounting Review*, May 617–652.

Ewert R and A Wagenhofer (2005). Economic effects of tightening accounting standards to restrict earnings management. *The Accounting Review*, October 1101–1124.

United States of America v. Jeffrey K Skilling and Kenneth L Lay, *Transcript of Proceedings Before the Honorable Sim Lake and a Jury.*

United States of America v. Jeffrey K Skilling and Kenneth L Lay, *Superseding Indictment*, Cr. No. H-04-25 (S-2) United States District Court, Southern District of Texas, Houston Division.

Chapter 17

Mark to Market Accounting:
Feeding the Growth Requirement

Mark to market accounting was one factor that brought on the collapse of Enron. Consider the following thought of Fox (2003, p. 311):

> As Enron showed, a company can become too focused on the short term, and one possible warning sign is an overreliance on mark-to-market accounting, especially in illiquid markets where values are based on internal assumptions.

Why is it that the accounting profession (including the SEC) allowed Enron to get so far off track? Basically, the profession failed to consider and apply its own history.

The Mark to Market Issue

Until recently, accounting was based on the use of historical costs. An asset was recorded at its cost. The cost could be written down or be expensed but an increase in value was not recorded.

Theoreticians pointed out the failings of a cost-based accounting system. Take an investor who paid $50 a share for the widely traded common stock of a large corporation. Time passes and the stock goes up to $90 a share. Should the $40 stock price appreciation be reported as a gain? Transaction costs and tax effects should be considered but most reasonable people would agree that a gain has taken place.

Now assume there are two investors and there is a cost-based accounting and no gain is recognized for accounting purposes unless there is a sale of the stock. But now assume one investor sells (with transaction costs equal to zero and no taxes). With the $90 of cash and a $40 gain, the investor now buys a share of stock. The stock is recorded at its $90 cost. The investor who does not sell has one share of stock with a cost of $40 and no gain. But the two shares of stock have the same value.

The consequence of the above cost-based accounting system is that the investor who wants a $40 gain cherry picks the portfolio by selling one share. The investor who does not want a gain in this accounting period does not sell. Obviously, a strict cost-based accounting, while well-defined, has major flaws.

The theoreticians pointed out that the crucial event in earning the $40 was not sale of the stock but rather the change in price. By marking the stock to market, the stock of all investors is recorded at $90 and a gain of $40 is recorded for all investors. This is superior to a system where the share may be recorded at $50 or $90 and a $40 gain may or may not be recorded.

Complexities

The above example is very persuasive about the merits of mark-to-market accounting. But now assume the investor owns a very large block of stock and the stock is not widely traded. While the current stock price can be read in the newspapers, the value that could be obtained for a large block of stock is not determined by the current market price. Estimating an effective market price for the share that represent a large percentage of the outstanding shares requires judgment.

Instead of an uncertain current price, there could be a problem estimating future prices as well as problems in discounting a future value estimate to obtain a present value equivalent.

In the case of Enron, traders would commit Enron to buy or sell natural gas many years in the future. If the contract was perfectly hedged, there still remained the problem of computing a present value. Also, many of the Enron contracts were not perfectly hedged.

The History

Paton and Littleton (1940) were not discussing Enron's specific accounting problems of 2001, but much of what they wrote before 1940 applies to the current accounting practices. First, they emphasized the need for verifiable objective evidence (p. 18):

> One of the important contributions made by professional auditing in its early development in Great Britain was the emphasis placed upon objective evidence to support recorded transactions. Recorded revenue was accepted as valid only on the basis of the objective evidence furnished by bona fide sales to independent parties; recorded expenditures were accepted as valid only on the basis of the objective evidence furnished by authentic business documents related to the transaction. This evidence afforded the principal means by which the recorded facts could be verified. The dependability of the accounts was thus subject to the test of an examination of the origin of the transactions recorded.

Most importantly, they stress the necessity of having objective evidence (p. 19):

> 'Objective' used here relates to the expression of facts without distortion from personal bias. It is in contrast to 'subjective,' a word which suggests that the personal equation — state of mind, wish, intent to deceive — may affect the result. 'Objective evidence' therefore is evidence which is impersonal and external to the person most concerned, in contrast with that person's unsupported opinion or desire.

The requirement for objective evidence is not absolute, thus we have (pp. 19–20):

> It is in connection with this subsequent treatment that the concept of objective determination must submit to some

variation, for 'objectively determined' is not a gauge that registers positive or negative and nothing more. The evidence supporting a given treatment may be completely objective, convincingly objective, doubtfully objective, or clearly unobjective.

It is clear that the Enron mark to market accounting practices were "clearly unobjective". Traders estimated future prices to a large extent based on the income outcome that was desired.

A Mark to Market Rule Target

In the spirit of Paton and Littleton (1940), let us consider some rules for mark to market accounting.

At one extreme, there are reliable current market prices for today (no time discounting). This is analogous to the common stock example for one share of stock. There is reliable objective evidence. In fact, we will call this the equivalent to certainty situation. When we have an equivalent to certainty situation, the mark to market accounting is not only acceptable, but it should be the required accounting method.

Now, let us consider the other extreme where there is a large amount of uncertainty. Assume that Ford Motor Company has just completed construction of an engine manufacturing plant at a cost of $200,000,000. The net present value of the plant at the time of construction was $700,000,000 (the total gross present value was $900,000,000). Should the plant be written up from $200,000,000 to $900,000,000?

The current practice for a manufacturing plant is for the plant's owner not to mark it up for future estimated cash flow. Even if there were a surge in property values so that the plant had an estimated value larger than $200,000,000 (the cost), this upsurge would not be recorded.

However, if the auto industry in the US were restructured and the estimated value of the plant was reduced to $30,000,000 (its value as a shopping mall), there could be a write down in value to $30,000,000.

Why was the plant not written up to $900,000,000 when that was its estimated present value? The $900,000,000 was highly uncertain and based on subjective estimates of value. With that degree of uncertainty, to report $700,000,000 of income because someone (or some group) thinks that in the future cash flows will be earned, would be to reduce significantly the usefulness of the firm's income statement.

We are now ready for a conclusion. Mark to market accounting should only be used when the information is objective and is applicable to the value estimate. When there is a large amount of uncertainty and the value calculation is based on subjective inputs from people who might well have a bias (a reason for preferring one accounting outcome over other accounting outcomes), then mark to market accounting is much less useful. If the amount of uncertainty is large, then it is possible that mark to market accounting is not a useful technique. The mark to market accounting may be useful for a corporation's internal use when it is not useful for external purposes (especially as the primary reporting device).

Let us consider the Enron situation where the firm signs a contract to deliver a quantity of natural gas each year at a given price for 20 years. Given today's natural gas price, the differential between the price to be received and the cost of buying the gas is $1,000,000 to be netted immediately.

To book the $1,000,000 as income is reasonable. There will be 19 additional net receipts or net outlays. To book $20,000,000 as income today is not reasonable. To book the present value of $1,000,000 a year for 20 years (say the present value is $9,365,000) is not necessarily correct. The correct discount rate might not be 0.10 and the amount each year might not be $1,000,000. In fact, the amount for one or more years might not be positive, they might be negative. Unless we know more than is assumed above, the recognition of the incomes of 2–20 years should not be published as known facts.

So far, we have stressed the difficulty of estimating the value of the contract for each year and choosing the correct discount rate, but there is also the bias (conscious or unconscious) of the person (or persons) doing the calculations. In the absence of the objective evidence required by Paton and Littleton, we cannot rely on the value estimates and the effects on income. Unfortunately, much of the inputs going into Enron's earnings numbers were based on estimates made by managers with something to gain or lose as the result of the income measures.

Feeding the Growth Requirement

When Jeff Skilling joined Enron, he insisted on the firm's use of mark to market accounting. He was concerned that the trading operations could arrange a contract with a value of $20,000,000 but only $2,000,000 was recognized as income under conventional accrual accounting since the revenues were not realized. Skilling probably did not appreciate the full consequences of using mark to market.

Consider a Wal-Mart type of retail firm that completes ten new stores at a cost of $20,000,000. It is expected that each year for 20 years the stores will earn $4,000,000 of cash flows. The present value of the cash flow is $34,054,000. Following conventional accounting rules for revenue recognition and assuming that the $4,000,000 of expected cash flows are earned, there will be $4,000,000 of earnings (adjusted downward for any accrual expenses not using cash flows) for year 1.

Assuming the same cash flows for each of the next 19 years, there will be comparable earnings each year. If one new store is completed in year 2, there will be growth in earnings for the firm.

Now assume the firm uses mark to market accounting. The present value of the ten stores is $34,054,000 which is $14,054,000 larger than the $20,000,000 cost. Assume the $14,054,000 value increment is recorded as income.

Now in year 2 there is a problem. Some time value income is reported in year 2 but basically something over ten new stores (not one) will have to be opened for there to be earnings growth. Mark to market accounting makes it difficult for there to be continuous earnings growth through time.

A Three Period Example

Assume a firm engages in a 3-year contract where the promise to supply natural gas is hedged by contracts to buy natural gas and the net value each year is $10,000,000. The firm uses a 0.10 time discount rate. The cash flows are received at the end of each year. The cash flows have a present value at time zero of $24,868,000.

			Present Value Factor		
Time	Cash flow	$(h1)^{-i}$	PV time 0	PV time 1	PV time 2
1	10,000,000	0.9091	$9,091,000		
2	10,000,000	0.8264	8,264,000	$9,091,000	
3	10,000,000	0.7513	7,513,000	8,264,000	$9,901,000
			$24,868,000	$17,355,000	$9,091,000

With mark to market accounting, the firm would have $24,868,000 of income for time 0 (the present value of the contracts).

At time 1, the value of 8,264,000 + 7,513,000 = $15,777,000 would have grown to 9,091,000 + 8,264,000 = 17,355,000. Thus, the income for year 2 is $1,578,000:

$$17,355,000 - 15,777,000 = \$1,578,000.$$

To maintain the income (avoid a decline in income), new contracts with a present value of $23,290,000 would have to be arranged.

$$24,868,000 - 1,578,000 = \$23,290,000.$$

In each year, new contracts would have to be arranged so that the income of the coming period beat the income of the period. With mark to market accounting, it is difficult to maintain income growth.

The Trial: Mark to Market

The trial consequences of Enron using mark to market accounting were all indirect. The US Attorneys did not attack the use or the application of mark to market by Enron. However, we can surmise that its use made it more difficult for Enron to meet its earnings and growth targets. Thus Ms Ruemmler states (p. 17714):

> Virtually every Government witness, ladies and gentlemen, told you that at Enron it was critically important for Enron to meet its earnings targets. There was tremendous pressure at Enron to generate earnings and hit earnings targets. Earnings were critical.

and (p. 17714):

> Mr Koenig told you, 'Earnings and earnings per share growth were the most important things that shareholders and investors looked at. If we missed by a penny, we thought the stock price would go down'.

There was concern that losses were not booked in a timely fashion:

> They were errors, errors in the contracts. They are losses. You can't just say, 'We're going to renegotiate them out later'. In mark-to-market accounting, as Ms Curry, who was the accountant, told you, the losses needed to be booked immediately.

Because the values recorded were estimates and the actual results were likely to be different than the estimates, reserves for value declines were recorded. But the amounts of reserves and their utilization was somewhat arbitrary (the Government argued, very arbitrary) (p. 17762):

> You also heard about reserves that were generated in the Enron North America business as a result of the trading business. You heard from Mr Colwell and Mr Delainey that 'Those reserves were inherently discretionary. There is all sorts of judgment involved. They can be easily manipulated, and it's very hard to detect'.

The use of the reserves was defined to be a crime (p. 17762):

> You know from Mr Koenig and Ms Rieker that the investing public was never told that Enron could pull a penny here, pull a penny there, for purposes of meeting the consensus estimate; that they would mess with the reserve or do some other kind of financial trickery in order to meet the consensus estimate.

The use of the reserves could be honest efforts by Enron to record complex financial transactions under conditions of uncertainty, or as alleged by the Government attempts by Enron (Skilling and Lay) to manipulate the firm's accounting results.

Conclusions

An axe used to chop down a dead tree is a useful tool. An axe used to harm a person may be a deadly weapon.

Mark to market accounting is analogous to the above axe. At the extreme case of certainty and complete objectivity, it tends to supply better information than cost-based accounting. But as the amount of uncertainty and the amount of subjectivity are increased, the positive aspects of mark to market accounting are reduced and it may actually be less useful than the old-fashioned cost-based accounting.

References

Fox, L (2003). *Enron: The Rise and Fall*. Hoboken, NJ: Wiley.

Paton, WA and AC Littleton (1940). *An Introduction to Corporate Accounting Standards*. Monograph No. 3. Ann Arbor, MI: American Accounting Association.

Chapter 18

Concluding Observations

We know that from August to December 2001, the newspapers reported many stories relating the wrongdoings of Enron. We also know that Skilling resigned the CEO job in August 2001 as the arrival of the bad news regarding Enron accelerated. Thereafter, Ken Lay took over as the CEO and was the CEO when Enron went bankrupt in December 2001.

In 2006, Skilling and Lay were brought to trial for fraud and related crimes (misleading investors, etc.). They were both found to be guilty. Lay died before sentencing and Skilling received a sentence of 24 years. To a large extent, subjective factors determined the guilt or innocence, thus reading the written record of the trial or reading this book is not sufficient to evaluate the accuracy of the verdicts.

What we can evaluate are the arguments and witnesses offered by the US Attorneys. The US Attorneys obviously used the fact that Skilling and Lay headed a firm whose bankruptcy caused many people to lose their life savings. We could argue that these investors in Enron should have had more diversification but the fact is that many of the small investors were not adequately diversified.

Judge Lake obviously considered the losses to investors in sentencing Skilling to 24 years in prison. Lake stated (*New York Times*, 24 October 2006)

> As the many victims have testified, his crimes have imposed on hundreds, if not thousands, a life sentence of poverty.

But it is never proven that Jeff Skilling caused Enron's bankruptcy. Most of his alleged crimes involved statements that were made in the interests of keeping Enron viable. At the sentencing, six Enron shareholders and former employees spoke in support of Skilling receiving the maximum sentence.

Andrew Fastow, the Chief Financial Officer of Enron, and the designer of the structures who led to Enron's demise received a sentence of six years.

If the Government was correct in charging Skilling and Lay with lying to project an inflated picture of Enron's health, then Skilling and Lay were probably doing everything they could to keep Enron alive. The actions of Skilling and Lay relative to the reporting of income did not cause Enron's demise. The loss of its ability to trade when it lost its investment grade rating was much more significant.

The US Attorneys had to make clear what specific crimes Skilling and Lay had committed. Too often, they essentially argued that these were evil men who had harmed too many relatively poor people.

The Trial

The prosecution fires a lot of shots hoping to hit something. Ms Ruemmler focuses on what she describes as the lies (some of the "lies" were excessive optimism or bad forecasts) (pp. 17698–17699):

> The Defendants are not charged with intending to cause the bankruptcy. Of course, they didn't set out by design — I can save the defense an argument. Of course, they didn't set out by design to cause the bankruptcy of the company. No one is alleging that they did that.
>
> What they are charged with is misleading and lying to the investing public for the two years leading up to Enron's collapse. That's what is at issue in the case, and that's what you need to focus on in your deliberations.

But all alleged lies were made in the interests of saving Enron and its stock. Skilling and Lay could have sold their entire stock holdings over the two-year period described by Ms Ruemmler.

There was no obvious criminal intent in the quoted statements of Skilling and Lay.

Of course, witnesses testified that bad things were done by Skilling and Lay. For example, continuing Ms Ruemmler's summary (pp. 17702–17703):

> Paula Rieker. You remember her. Corporate secretary. Number two person, investor relations. Mark Koenig, the head of investor relations, the very first witness in the case. Mr Glisan, Mr Delainey, Mr Colwell, Mr Loehr. These people are not career criminals, ladies and gentlemen, they're human beings. They're people with families. Mothers, fathers. Sadly, they also broke the law. Do you think for one second, for one second, it was easy for those people to come in here, to sit up on that witness stand in this very, very public trial and say, 'I committed fraud at Enron'? Do you think that was easy for them? To have to tell their friends and their neighbors and their family members that they had accepted responsibility for what they had done, to admit that they had broken the law? You saw them.

Let us consider the situation of Ms P Rieker. Ms Rieker pleaded guilty (2004) to insider trading. She sold Enron shares when she learned Enron's broadband business had lost more money than had been forecasted. This is a crime, trading on insider information. Martha Stewart went to jail because the Government suspected she traded on insider information (she actually was convicted of lying to investigators).

On 7 October 2006, in exchange for "cooperation", Paula H Rieker was sentenced to two years of probation instead of ten years in prison. She was the former corporate secretary and an executive in the investor relations department.

This is not meant to imply that Ms Rieker's testimony was not an honest interpretation of what transpired. But it does suggest that Ms Rieker did have a real incentive to have her testimony appear to be consistent with the Government's case. The power of the US Government unleashed in a court room is frightening.

Ms Ruemmler concludes that Skilling and Lay lied and did so to serve their own interests (p. 17705):

> They had choices to put the investors' and employees' interests ahead of their own or to put themselves first. Time and time again, they chose to put themselves first. By withholding information that the investors were entitled to, they deprived those people. They had a special duty, special obligation. They got special compensation for those duties.

Remember it is alleged that Skilling and Lay knew Enron was a bad investment for two years and hid that fact by lying to serve their own financial interests.

But if Ms Ruemmler is right on this, why did Skilling and Lay not sell the majority of their shares long before the summer of 2001? It makes no sense for both of them to hold Enron shares to the extent they did if they knew it was a bad investment. The fact is that the logic of the situation implies that both Skilling and Lay thought Enron was a good investment right up to September 2001 (and possibly beyond). The intent to defraud would seem to be missing (but necessary for conviction).

How could they refute all the accusations to crimes? Consider Ms Ruemmler's summary of the Raptors (remember there were four Raptors, each somewhat different (p. 17707)):

> Let me just give you an example. Let's talk about some of the transactions we've heard something about. The Raptors. What's the cover story? The cover story is that, well, these were all approved by Arthur Andersen, by lawyers. You saw, you have them in evidence, thousands, I think, pages of documents to make the Raptors look

legit. They were just typical financing structures. Mr. Lay told investors that they were so insignificant that he wasn't even sure that they had a name.

The implication was that the Raptors were illegal and needed a cover story. The Raptors were not illegal. SPEs were widely used by a wide range of corporations.

Now, Enron had a problem with the accounting for its SPEs. Consider EITF Abstracts (Issue No. 85-1) of 28 March 1985.[a]

ISSUE

An enterprise receives a note, rather than cash, as a contribution to its equity. The transaction may be a sale of capital stock or a contribution to paid-in capital.

The issue is whether an enterprise should report the note receivable as a reduction of shareholders' equity or as an asset.

EITF DISCUSSION

The Task Force reached a consensus that reporting the note as an asset is generally not appropriate, except in very limited circumstances when there is substantial evidence of ability and intent to pay within a reasonably short period of time. Some Task Force members would require collateralization, or payment of the note prior to issuance of the financial statements, to permit asset recognition.

The SEC requires that public companies report notes received in payment for the enterprise's stock as a deduction from shareholders' equity. Task Force members confirmed that the predominant practice is to offset the notes and stock in the equity section. However, such notes may be recorded as an asset if collected in cash prior to issuance of the financial statements.

[a] EITF translates to Emerging Issues Task Force.

Because the Enron accountants were not aware of Issue No. 85-1, they made a $1.2 billion error and increased stock equity by $1.2 billion. There were many accountants not aware of Issue No. 85-1 before September 2001 when the world became aware of Enron's mistake.

Compared to the 3% of independent equity SEC rule for not consolidating SPEs, the Issue No. 85-1 was common knowledge. Nonaccountants were completely in the dark regarding the 3% rule. But the use of a nonconsolidated SPE is not a crime.

Note that I am not discussing Cuiaba in detail. If Skilling told Fastow that Skilling (and Enron) would not allow Fastow to lose money on investing in Cuiaba, then treating the sale of Enron's investment to a Raptor as a sale would be wrong (Enron stands ready to buy back the investment). In this case, the jury must decide who is telling the truth. Remember Fastow's sentence is reduced from ten years to six years as a result of his testimony.

Mr Berkowitz (US Attorney) thought that Fastow was locked into ten years and had no hope of a reduction in sentence (p. 18265):

> You go back and you review your notes. That document was produced after Mr Fastow had his 10-year deal. It was produced after his wife had entered into her final plea agreement. The only thing that that document could do, ladies and gentlemen, was sink him if it were a fraud. The deals were already in place. Ten years locked in for Mr Fastow. His wife's deal done. No possible reason that he would come forward with a document that wasn't accurate.

Berkowitz was wrong. Fastow got his sentence reduced to six years.

Berkowitz also objected to Enron being described by Lay as a logistics company rather than as a speculator (p. 18281):

> 'You know, some people have said Enron's a trading business. Let me hit that one head on. We are not a trading business. We are a logistics company'. He was telling the market, ladies and gentlemen, that volumes

were what drove the profitability, essentially, like their Toyota. 'Every car we sell, we're making a gross margin on that. We build it for a thousand dollars. We sell it for $2,000. That's what goes on. Each piece of gas we sell, we're making a margin. That's how we're making our money, ladies and gentlemen. You can sleep well. It's going to be sustainable. It's consistent'.

He did not tell them that they were making their money speculative trading, but that's what the truth was, ladies and gentlemen.

A group of experts could argue all day long as to whether Enron was a trading company, a logistics company, or a speculating company. There would be no agreement until the question was asked as to which position was a crime. On this, there would be no argument. No crime to choose one of the three.

The Pro forma Earnings

The ROEs of Enron for 1998–2001 are surprisingly modest (less than 10% per year). This implies that Enron was not a profitable operation. But this is misleading.

Consider the SPEs of Fastow where the equity investors earned in excess of 30% per year. If the 30% earned by the SPEs is imputed to Enron and the real return earned for Enron by the SPEs is subtracted, one would guess that the ROE of Enron would easily exceed 10%. We do not have the information to do the above calculations, but the adjustment would be interesting.

The Jaedicke Factor

The strongest argument that can be made that Skilling and Lay did not fully understand Fastow's use of SPEs is the Chairman of Enron's Audit Committee of the Board of Directors, Robert K Jaedicke, was fooled (Bob is a good friend of the author). Jaedicke is very smart, very knowledgeable about accounting, hard working, and most importantly completely honest. If Fastow could get his crimes past him, he could easily get them past Skilling and Lay. I do not know that Skilling and Lay did not see through Fastow sufficiently, but we know that Jaedicke was faked out.

The Arthur Andersen Memorial Award

James B Stewart nominated Jeffrey Skilling and Keneth Lay for the Arthur Andersen "award for worst white-collar defense of the year". The award "seeks to recognize a defense strategy so ill-conceived that even an innocent defendant would run the risk of ending up in jail or out of business" (see *The Wall Street Journal*, 31 May 2006).

Stewart writes that Lay wins the award.

> He undermined his own reputation as a benevolent civic leader in minutes, alternatively displaying arrogance and self-righteousness.

Other observers have also indicated that Lay's performance as a witness was very bad. But I think Stewart missed a major point. The US Attorneys prosecuting the cases were brilliant and heartless in doing whatever was necessary to gain convictions. I would praise the prosecution for their strategies to gain conviction rather than be critical of the defense attorneys. Now, I must admit to disagreeing with the tactics used to gain the convictions, but that is a matter of my definition of the appropriate objectives for the US Government.

The Ostrich Defense

Judge Lake gave instructions to the Skilling–Lay jury that allowed jurors to find Skilling and Lay guilty because they consciously avoided knowing about the wrongdoings at Enron. Lay obviously had no interest in the accounting and finance complexities that Fastow was constructing (he did not consciously avoid the issues). Skilling, on the other hand, did not claim not to know what was going on.

The Appeals Court will have a lot of issues to consider.

The Amount of Loss

Investors in the common stock attribute their losses to Skilling. The *Wall Street Journal* (24 October 2006) reported the following:

> 'Give him what he deserves: the rest of his life in prison', said Anne Beliveaux, an 18-year Enron veteran who was an administrative assistant at the company. She said she lost more than $500,000 when the value of the company's stock collapsed.

First, consider that Skilling did all he could to avoid having the Enron stock collapse. Second, if Skilling had not pumped up the stock price (as charged by the government), Anne's loss would have been much less than $500,000, since the stock would not have been high enough to have her investment reach $500,000 of value.

The Reasons Enron Failed

The Government convinced the Skilling and Lay jury in 2006 that Skilling and Lay caused the Enron bankruptcy. Stewart (2006) does a much better job of identifying the causes of Enron's fall. My words follow not Stewart's, but the primary thoughts are his for the first four items.

1. The focus on growth in earnings-per-share, rather than more useful measures.
2. Management and others had the wrong incentives.
3. Use of mark-to-market accounting (as described in previous chapters).
4. Closing the deal was more important than operating the asset profitably. Closing the deal was rewarded financially more than operating the assets.

He could have added to his short list that Lay let good people leave and promoted people who ultimately destroyed the company.

Too often, Enron bought its way into activities (e.g., water) and locations (e.g., Brazil, India, England, and Argentina) that it did not understand.

To raise money quickly Enron frequently offered an arrangement where the loans could require payment when a trigger event was breached. During the fall of 2001 these triggers caused premature debt payments and resulting financial crises.

Lay's outside interests caused him to be distracted and not concerned adequately with important details of managing Enron.

Maybe Fastow could not be managed by anything less than a full time keeper. When Fastow's activities were made public the investing community concluded that the entire Enron operations were flawed rather than just a small segment. The fact that the major real operations were intact and profitable was ignored. A trading firm's operations must be transparent and solid financially so that the firm can be rated in the investment grade.

Conclusions

The guilt and innocence of Skilling and Lay will be argued by well-qualified lawyers for many future decades. Was there criminal intent? What was Lay's criminal intent and motivation in September to December 2001? That he was overly optimistic is easily shown by the sequence of events.

Even Fastow was probably not aware that he was committing crimes. He was having fun playing games and getting rich. His intent was probably not to break the law.

The Enron managers should have been stopped (they were). They should have been fined (they were).

Sending Skilling to jail for a long period of time for the things he did is not something that history will look back on favorably.

The US Attorneys "knew" that these people at Enron had committed outrageous crimes that used marginal techniques to gain convictions. This is also wrong.

Eichenwald (2005) argues that Enron is less a tale of criminals than a "Conspiracy of Fools". I am not sure it was a conspiracy, but I suspect too many of the participants were fools or alternatively acted foolishly.

A Postscript

On 8 September 2007, both *The New York Times* and *The Wall Street Journal* reported that the lawyers of Jeffrey K Skilling had asked the United States Court of Appeals in New Orleans to throw out his convictions on 19 charges. At a minimum, Mr Skilling would probably hope to reduce the 24-year sentence so that he could be transferred to a much less severe prison. Also, he probably would like to retain some or all of his $45 million assets.

He is likely to have some success in his appeal and maybe a large amount of success. Daniel Petrocelli, one of Mr Skilling's lawyers stated "he is very hopeful about the prospects for a complete reversal, as are we" (*The Wall Street Journal*, 8 September 2007). We shall see.

References

Eichenwald, K (2005). *Conspiracy of Fools*. New York: Broadway Books.
Stewart, B (2006). The real reasons Enron failed. *Journal of Applied Corporate Finance*, 18, 116–119.

Index